TURNING THE
WORLD
UPSIDE DOWN

D1412294

TURNING THE WORLD UPSIDE DOWN

Kenneth F. Haney
& Robin Johnston, editors

Turning the World Upside Down

Kenneth F. Haney, Robin Johnston, editors

©Copyright 2008 United Pentecostal Church International
Hazelwood, MO 63042-2299

Cover design by Laura Jurek

ISBN 0-7577-3699-5

Unless otherwise indicated, all quotations of Scripture are from The King James Version of the Bible.

Printed in the United States of America

Printed by

WORD AFLAME PRESS
8855 Dunn Road, Hazelwood, MO 63042
www.pentecostalpublishing.com

TABLE OF CONTENTS

INTRODUCTION

The first century church was an aggressive church. Evangelism was its heartbeat. That heartbeat compelled Paul to invade Europe with the gospel. When he and Silas arrived in the city of Thessalonica the Jewish leaders complained, "These that have turned the world upside down are come hither also" (Acts 17:6).

The world needs to be turned upside down again. It needs to hear the clarion call of the gospel. The good news is that the United Pentecostal Church International stands poised to take her commitment to evangelism and discipleship to the next level. The Global Impact initiative is designed to be a help to make this dream a reality.

This book is a collaborative effort of ten leaders within the United Pentecostal Church International designed to share their insights about how to achieve the lofty goals of the Global Impact initiative. Like the Global Impact initiative itself, this book is the brainchild of General Superintendent Kenneth F. Haney. He not only chose the contributors and their subjects, he wrote the opening chapter of the volume. His chapter reiterates the role vision plays in the accomplishment of a goal. He is at his best when casting a vision.

David K. Bernard, pastor of New Life Church, Austin, Texas, and district superintendent of the South Texas District, wrote the second chapter in the collection. He takes a look at what fueled the amazing growth of the first century apostolic church. He distills his findings into concepts that are applicable to today's church.

In chapter 3 Robin Johnston, associate editor of the UPCI and curator of the Center for the Study of Oneness Pentecostalism, shares some lessons that can be learned from the founders of the modern Pentecostal movement. He suggests that the church can be well served by looking back at what ignited the early Pentecostal revival while still looking to new opportunities that challenge the contemporary church.

Jerry Jones, general secretary of the UPCI, writes forcefully about the value of doctrine. In chapter 4 he implores the church to proclaim the truth. Strong churches are built on doctrine, and contrary to the opinion of some, doctrine is not a hindrance to the development of a growing church.

Jerry Dillon, pastor of Parkway Pentecostal Church in Madison, Mississippi, is defined by passion. In chapter 5, he writes of the critical need of a passion for the gospel. Lethargy is the nemesis of passion and it blunts the vigor of the church. Passion attracts people to the gospel.

Randy Keyes is the pastor of Revival Center United Pentecostal Church in Modesto, California, and the assistant general superintendent of the UPCI. His contribution to the book is a timely message on the value of separation. A holy God desires a holy people. Separation, properly taught, is attractive to those seeking a life-changing encounter with God.

Chapter 8 was written by Carlton Coon Sr., the general director of the Home Missions Division. He highlights the priority of unity both to the church and more importantly to Jesus. After all, Jesus prayed that we might all be one. The chapter discusses the contours of unity and closes with a sample covenant designed to promote unity.

Bruce Howell, general director of the Foreign Missions Division, writes on the supernatural. The chapter is filled with miracle stories and it issues a challenge to the reader not to overlook the importance of the supernatural in the conception and development of an apostolic revival.

Paul Mooney, pastor of Calvary Tabernacle, Indianapolis, Indiana, and an assistant general superintendent of the UPCI, penned chapter 9. This chapter draws attention to the urgency of the moment in which we live. The church needs to make a "final thrust" before the coming of the Lord.

The final chapter of the book was written by Jack Cunningham, pastor of Bible World Church, Chesapeake, Virginia, and district superintendent of the Virginia District. He moves the book from theory to practice. This chapter lays out the master plan for the Global Impact initiative. It gives a workable roadmap for the local church's involvement with the initiative. The key to Global Impact is local impact.

Turning the World Upside Down offers a challenge to the United Pentecostal Church International. The writers offer their thoughts of how to meet the challenge. You must decide if you are willing to accept the challenge.

VISION

by Kenneth F. Haney

"Where there is no vision, the people perish" *(Proverbs 29:18).*

In the beginning, God had a vision for His church. It was a positive vision. When Jesus founded the church, they were *one* in unity, *one* in doctrine, *one* in holiness, and *one* in Spirit. (See Acts 2.) They were bonded with a common cause: that of fulfilling the great commission. The enemy worked, even as he does now, at fragmenting unity, bringing division, introducing false doctrines, and destroying holiness. Satan's plan has been to prevent the church from becoming *one*. He is the author of division, the opposite of vision. He works at causing schism in the body of Christ.

The magnitude of the revival God desires to send in these latter times cannot be housed in church buildings. When Jesus talked about the church, He was not referring to structures—mortar, brick, steel, chandeliers, carpets, and stained glass windows. He meant *people*! The whole purpose of His coming into the world was to give Himself as a sacrifice or ransom for mankind. Matthew Henry states: "It [the church] is a number of the children of men called out of the world, and set apart from it, and dedicated to Christ."

The construction of beautiful church buildings says something to a community, and that is important, but we must remember that the original church in Jerusalem began without its own building. It exploded into existence in an upper room. One hundred and twenty were filled with the Holy Spirit. They spoke in tongues, which were accompanied by the sound of a rushing mighty wind and cloven tongues as of fire! This was the beginning of the church. From this initial infilling, the church grew to three thousand, then to five thousand, and then to multitudes. Soon they were accused of filling Jerusalem with their doctrine. Most historians agree that the church in Jerusalem numbered somewhere between sixty thousand to eighty thousand firm believers shortly after the first century.

A building could not be built that would house this many people. It happened so quickly that it was very important for the church, under the leadership of the Bishop James, to be organized in order to accommodate the great harvest that the Lord had sent. They expected growth and revival and believed for it. It was in the very fiber of their being; it dominated their thoughts and actions.

In many cases today, we have limited God and tied His hands by speaking negative thoughts and talking more about those who have fallen from the faith and the apostates of the latter time, than about what God will do about the harvest in the end time. Our minds can become so cluttered by the environment of our times, that all we can see is the deterioration, judgment, and the annihilation of the human race. We must be careful not to miss the whole purpose for the existence of these circumstances. Current events have been permitted by God so that the church can do its greatest work in this final hour.

Power of Vision

Vision is not a choice. Most people have visions or pictures in their minds, but what is the vision God wants us to have? Vision is an image of the future, something forthcoming.

What affects our vision? Our environment, what we read, what we see, what we hear, the people with whom we associate, the time we choose to spend in talking to the Lord—all these things affect our vision.

Vision needs to be "caught" from the spirit of the early church, and not by comparing ourselves with each other. Comparing ourselves among ourselves is one of the greatest downfalls of our time. In so doing we not only do not do well (II Corinthians 10:12), but we also inhibit the Word of God from going forward. Many have adopted ideas and concepts for church growth developed in the twentieth century. What we need to do is revert back to the New Testament church found in the Book of Acts and the Epistles. There we see how God blessed and multiplied churches with a tremendous earthshaking revival.

We have been quick to adopt the methods and patterns of modern day denominational churches, while equally as quick to condemn the heresy and false doctrine that they may embrace. Along with contending for the faith that was once delivered to the saints, and holding to the biblical truth of the Scriptures, it is equally important that we follow New Testament procedures and methods for church growth.

This is our day! Shakespeare wrote, "There is a tide in the affairs of men which, taken at the flood, leads on to fortune; omitted, all the voyage of their life is bound in shallows and in miseries; we must take the current when it serves or lose our venture" (*Julius Caesar*, Act IV).

There is also a tide in the affairs of God. We will take to the current. Entire congregations are being, and will continue to be, baptized in the wonderful name of Jesus and filled with His Spirit!

God has great vision for the church; we must get in sync with His vision!

We All Have Vision

Whether good or bad, positive or negative, we all have vision! We all have images in our minds. The Bible is replete with examples of both good and bad vision. Contrast the image of the ten spies, who in their own eyes looked like grasshoppers, with Joshua and Caleb, who said of the land of Caanan, "We are well able to overcome it" (Numbers 13:30-33). Gideon, even though he wondered about it, believed in God's vision of winning a battle against thousands with only three hundred men.

Right vision or image will affect the purity of the heart. When David was running with negative talkers, he said, "I shall now perish one day by the hand of Saul" (I Samuel 27:1). David was not going to perish. He was anointed to be the king. Paul understood the influence of image when he said, "Casting down imaginations, and every high thing that exalteth itself against the knowledge of God, and bringing into captivity every thought to the obedience of Christ" (II Corinthians 10:5).

In the natural realm, the Wright brothers, Alexander Graham Bell, and Thomas Edison, all great inventors, began with an imaginative idea that came from their minds. Imagination sows the seeds of reality.

What image is in your heart? Jesus said, "Out of the abundance of the heart the mouth speaketh" (Matthew

12:34). The image in your heart is what you speak, think, and signal to those around you. Either we create the atmosphere conducive for God to work, or we allow the enemy to work against us. It is important to preach, sing, talk, live, act, and envision right images so that victory will come. Live the Word, not your feelings, and the result follows!

The element of faith is essential in obtaining vision, and without vision, the victory of life can never be achieved. The vision must be believed. "And seek not ye what ye shall eat, or what ye shall drink, neither be ye of doubtful mind" (Luke 12:29). A doubtful mind demonstrates a lack of faith.

This doubt was demonstrated in the Old Testament story of Elisha at Dothan. His servant said, "Alas, my master! What shall we do?" Fear was a natural response—but there is something bigger than fear. Elisha could see something in the realm of the Spirit that the servant could not see and responded with these words: "Fear not: for they that be with us are more than they that be with them" (II Kings 6:16). The servant saw the enemy; Elisha saw God!

After he had spoken these words, Elisha told his servant to go take another look. It would be good for us to take another look when things seem impossible. Sometimes all one can see and hear is the neighing of the horses, the bustling of the enemy's chariots, and the enemies of God declaring war against the church. Remember that man's extremities are God's opportunities. When the servant took the second look, the Lord opened his eyes to see the innumerable angelic host.

In Mark 5, Jairus, the ruler of the synagogue, sought Jesus to heal his sick daughter who was nigh unto death. God's power was greater than the circumstances. Before Christ arrived at the house, a messenger came and told the ruler that it was not necessary to bother Jesus, for the daughter had already died. When Jesus heard what the servant spoke to the ruler, He said, "Be not afraid, only believe" (Mark 5:36).

Before they had even reached the doorstep of the home, they heard the wailing and the crying that confirmed the death of the daughter. But when Jesus stepped into the home, He said, "The damsel is not dead, but sleepeth" (Mark 5:39). They laughed Him to scorn. They looked upon Jesus as just another religious leader. If we are not careful, we will look upon ourselves as just another denomination. We are more than that! We are the church, the New Testament church, the church of the living God. We must do what Jesus did.

We Choose Our Vision

Each pastor will choose his or her vision. It is the will of God to send great revival through the medium of His church. The local church is where the revival must start if the world is to be touched. The vision must be greater than the negative voices around us.

The local church is the key to revival, and the pastor is the key to the local church. There seems little hope of reviving some congregations unless the minister can first be revived. The pastor can block revival or bless revival. He is a man under authority and with authority. The Bible speaks about him being a star in the right hand of Jesus (Revelation 1:20).

The seven letters in Revelation, found in chapters 2 and 3, are letters to individual churches. Most of them are revival messages to the congregations, and when God wants to talk to the church, He talks to the minister, the *angel* of the church. In each case, if the pastor gets the message, the church will get it also. Every pastor must first catch the vision, then ask God for an anointing to reach his congregation and infuse them with a fire of passion to reach every soul by whatever method they can use to impart the truth!

As a pastor approaching a new year, I would seek God and ask Him for a vision for that year. He would put the vision into my heart. Often I found His will for the people burning in my spirit. Of course, I would write it all down, prepare banners, sometimes PowerPoints, and often print brochures or booklets laying out the vision. On the first Sunday of the new year we would present the vision. It often became the most exciting service of the year. I would ask the Lord to anoint me like never before so that the people would indeed catch the vision, for without them we could not succeed. In the midst of the presentation message we would worship, pray, and sometimes shout as the children of Israel did as they marched around the walls of Jericho. It was truly an exciting thing, but more importantly, I knew the people must buy into the pastor's vision in order for it to succeed.

Years ago someone gave me a plaque with a statement by William Carey: "Attempt great things for God, expect great things from God." The first century church attempted great and mighty things for God. As a result they likewise expected great acts from the Lord. They *believed* they could change the world. There was not a question in their minds that the world could be changed, if they were willing to pay the price. They did not permit negative thoughts to enter their minds. They believed every city, every village, and every country they entered into would be affected by the gospel. Night and day they lived with confidence that the world would be turned upside down through the apostolic ministry.

We Persevere to Keep the Vision

If you are a man or woman of God, He will speak to you and give you dreams and visions for the people you are responsible to lead. No matter what happens, remember God keeps His promises. If He made a promise to you or gave you a vision, it shall come to pass if you persevere. It is imperative to persevere even though it looks like the vision will be stamped out or obliterated. God made a promise to Abraham, but it took years to come to pass. Centuries later, Stephen spoke before the high priest and the council about this promise: "But when the time of the promise drew nigh, which God had sworn to Abraham, the people grew and multiplied in Egypt" (Acts 7:17).

A spirit of doubt permeates the atmosphere of the last days. "Knowing this first, that there shall come in the last days scoffers, walking after their own lusts, and saying, Where is the promise of his coming? for since the fathers fell asleep, all things continue as they were from the beginning of the creation" (II Peter 3:3-4).

It is imperative that we keep the promise of our vision alive. Following are the temptations that visionaries face:

1. *The temptation to take shortcuts.* The devil wanted Jesus to take a shortcut and subvert the perfect will of God. (See Matthew 4.) In the case of Sarah and Abraham, Sarah took a shortcut and told her husband to have a child with the bondwoman. There has been war ever since between the two nations that are the offspring of Sarah and Hagar.

2. *The temptation to give up.* Many have given up their vision because of the long struggle that hindered them from attaining their goal. If they would have just persevered, they would have attained their vision.

3. *The temptation to deny the origin of the dream.* It is possible to doubt and say, "Maybe it was not God; maybe it was just my imagination." Never give up God's promise. Be like Abraham and stagger not. "He staggered not at the promise of God through unbelief; but was strong in faith, giving glory to God" (Romans 4:20).

4. *The temptation of pride.* A little success can produce a lust for power and evoke self-pride. Some people begin humble and dependent upon God, but they cannot handle the successes and blessings of the Lord. This spirit was in King Nebuchadnezzar. When he walked in the palace, he was filled with pride. "The king spake, and said, Is not this great Babylon, that I have built for the house of the kingdom by the might of my power, and for the honour of my majesty?" (Daniel 4:30). While the word was in his mouth, God stripped him of his kingdom and drove him into the wilds to live as a wild beast. We must never cease to give all glory to God.

5. *The temptation to settle for almost.* We must have endurance for everything God has promised and not settle for less. Almost is not enough! What God has promised He will perform!

Temptation came to Joseph. He lost two coats: one to his brethren and one to a seducing woman. Joseph knew who his real audience was. It was not the people; it was

God. Joseph even lost his name but kept his dream. You may lose your coat but do not lose your dream.

God gave Moses a dream of a Promised Land. Moses allowed his frustration and anger to abort the dream. God told him to speak to the rock and water would come forth, but Moses struck the rock instead. "And the LORD spake unto Moses and Aaron, Because ye believed me not, to sanctify me in the eyes of the children of Israel, therefore ye shall not bring this congregation into the land which I have given them" (Numbers 20:12).

The apostle Paul knew the importance of keeping the vision. He said, "I was not disobedient unto the heavenly vision" (Acts 26:19). Keeping the vision was not without sufferings. "Of the Jews five times received I forty stripes save one. Thrice was I beaten with rods, once was I stoned, thrice I suffered shipwreck, a night and a day I have been in the deep; in journeyings often, in perils of waters, in perils of robbers, in perils by mine own countrymen, in perils by the heathen, in perils in the city, in perils in the wilderness, in perils in the sea, in perils among false brethren; in weariness and painfulness, in watchings often, in hunger and thirst, in fastings often, in cold and nakedness. Beside those things that are without, that which cometh upon me daily, the care of all the churches" (II Corinthians 11:24-28).

Not only did Paul suffer all of the above; he was buffeted by Satan, who sent a thorn in the flesh. God allowed it to be so Paul would not be exalted above measure. When God said, "My grace is sufficient for thee; for my strength is made perfect in weakness," Paul simply answered: "Most gladly therefore will I rather glory in my infirmities, that the power of Christ may rest upon me. Therefore I take pleasure in infirmities, in reproaches, in necessities, in persecutions, in distresses for Christ's sake: for when I am weak, then am I strong" (II Corinthians 12:9-10).

Paul was looking past the curtain of time, beyond the veil of flesh. I remember the old song Odell Cagle used to sing:

Let me look past the curtain of sorrow and tears
Let me view that sunny bright clime
It will strengthen my faith and will banish my fears
Let me look past the curtain of time.

Our Vision Determines Our Destiny

Vision will affect our destiny for good or for bad. In Moses' time, the vision of the people caused them not only to wander forty years in the wilderness, but even to die there, never attaining the vision God had for them. In Joshua's time, their vision caused them to see the walls of Jericho coming down. One had victory, the other had failure. In Moses' time they existed, but they never conquered, all because of their vision!

It is imperative that the church takes every positive step possible in the direction of preparing for the great harvest that is already waiting. God is sending a mighty ingathering of souls in the end.

In the last days, judgment is coming. The signs of the times are declared daily in the news. Paul and Jesus both spoke of the "falling away," but also simultaneous with this "falling away" is prophesied revival, harvest, and revelation of truth. All of the negative situations of the last days are in the process of preparing the hearts of men for the *greatest* ingathering of all times, which will continue among the children of Israel after the church is raptured.

21

The vision of the hour is "I will pour out my spirit upon all flesh" (Joel 2:28). There will be a revival among *backsliders*: prodigal sons and daughters will come home. This is revival! The revelation of the *one true God* and baptism in Jesus' name will spread throughout the world. Many trinitarian ministers are and will continue to receive this revelation.

The United Pentecostal Church International was birthed for this hour. We are to carry this message to the world! We must catch the *vision* and fulfill God's plan for the hour. Pastor, you have been placed in your city by God. You are not an accident. Do whatever it takes to reach every community of the city. Think outside of the box. Most people will not come into your church. You must go to them. Send buses into their neighborhoods. Teach them Bible studies. Rent one-room offices or storefronts to meet with them. Organize small groups to meet in multiple locations. Fast, pray, receive God's vision and plan.

Jesus spent three and one-half years casting His vision for the world and for His church. After His death, resurrection, and ascension, that vision was launched on the Day of Pentecost. That vision was an obsession for His followers and they were empowered by the Spirit. They did not just have the Holy Ghost, the Holy Ghost had them, and they were driven by the vision. They could see a conquered world and there was no foe that could defeat them. They suffered, were beaten, incarcerated, and martyred, but they kept subduing kingdoms and conquering cities. All the apostles were martyred with the exception of John, but that did not stop the church. They were driven by the power of Christ's vision and were equipped with passion to spread His gospel.

In the Book of Acts they converted everyone. The Thessalonians testified, "These that have turned the world upside down are come hither also" (Acts 17:6). They aggressively spread the gospel. "And this continued by the space of two years; so that all they which dwelt in Asia heard the word of the Lord Jesus, both Jews and Greeks" (Acts 19:10). Historians tell us that by the end of the second century one-half of the known world embraced the apostolic doctrine. The power of God and their vision enabled them to convert the world to this apostolic message!

Satan has deceived many men and women of God by convincing them that they will not succeed in reaching their cities. They have a negative image of the church; thus they have lived with disappointments. However, it is high time to change our image. How can this happen? Through prayer, fasting, and faith in God's Word! Ask God to give you a new picture, image, or vision. See the church filled with visitors! See yourself anointed and preaching with great unction. See the altars filled with hungry men and women, mothers and fathers, teenagers and children crying out to God. See a Book of Acts revival! Why not dream big?

Jesus' vision was GLOBAL: "For God so loved the world, that He gave" (John 3:16). Thus the vision of His church must be GLOBAL. The vision for the United Pentecostal Church International is GLOBAL IMPACT! It is a grassroots vision that affects all of the Jesus Name people from children to teenagers to adults, from the smallest to the largest of churches, from continent to continent, from nation to nation, and from city to city. The whole world must and will be mightily impacted by this apostolic message. We, His church, are all *involved*. We must be obsessed with the vision to reach a lost WORLD!

THE BLUEPRINT

by David K. Bernard

"And they continued steadfastly in the apostles' doctrine and fellowship, in the breaking of bread, and in prayers.... And the Lord added to the church daily those who were being saved" (Acts 2:42, 47). (Scripture quotations are from the NKJV.)

The New Testament church of the first century is our blueprint for revival and church growth today. To be part of the church of Jesus Christ and to have true spiritual growth, we must adhere to the message and experience of the apostles. Only then can we grow "with the increase that is from God" (Colossians 2:19).

Jesus Christ established the New Testament church by the apostles He had chosen. When He commissioned them to preach the gospel, He told them, "He who receives you receives Me." (See Matthew 10:1-7, 40). Shortly before His crucifixion, He prayed for the apostles and then said, "I do not pray for these alone, but also for those who will believe in Me through their word" (John 17:20). The church is "built on the foundation of the apostles and prophets, Jesus Christ Himself being the chief cornerstone" (Ephesians 2:20).

In Acts 2, we find the following essential characteristics of the New Testament church, which we need today if we are to be apostolic:

- *Apostolic experience*: "And they were all filled with the Holy Spirit and began to speak with other tongues, as the Spirit gave them utterance.... Then those who gladly received his word were baptized; and that day about three thousand souls were added to them" (verses 4, 41).
- *Apostolic doctrine*: "And they continued steadfastly in the apostles' doctrine" (verse 42). The apostolic message included the true humanity of Jesus Christ (verses 22, 30); the true deity of Jesus Christ (verse 36); the gospel of the death, burial, and resurrection of Jesus Christ for our salvation (verses 22-36); the personal response to the gospel by repentance, water baptism in the name of Jesus Christ for the remission of sins, and receiving the gift of the Holy Spirit (verses 37-39); and the life of holiness (verse 40).
- *Apostolic unity and fellowship*: "When the Day of Pentecost had fully come, they were all with one accord in one place.... And they continued steadfastly in the apostles' doctrine and fellowship, in the breaking of bread.... Now all who believed were together, and had all things in common, and sold their possessions and goods, and divided them among all, as anyone had need. So continuing daily with one accord in the temple, and breaking bread from house to house, they ate their food with gladness and simplicity of heart" (verses 1, 42, 44-46). The

pooling of all resources was a temporary practice by the thousands of new believers from many towns and countries who had traveled to Jerusalem for the Feast of Pentecost and remained there after receiving the Holy Spirit, probably in anticipation of the soon return of Jesus. As time went on, the believers scattered, established congregations in many locations, and instituted a different financial system (I Corinthians 9:3-14; 16:2). Nevertheless the principle remained the same—giving generously with one accord as God enables, to meet the needs of the body (II Corinthians 8-9).

- *Apostolic prayer and praise*: "And they continued steadfastly ... in prayers.... So continuing daily with one accord in the temple, and breaking bread from house to house, they ate their food with gladness and simplicity of heart, praising God and having favor with all the people" (verses 42, 46-47).
- *Apostolic miracles*: "Then fear came upon every soul, and many wonders and signs were done through the apostles" (verse 43).

The result was consistent church growth: "And the Lord added to the church daily those who were being saved" (Acts 2:47). If we will follow these principles, we can expect the same results. If we fail to implement these principles, we may still have some results, perhaps even spectacular results, but we will not have authentic church growth. Our goal must be to see both *quantitative growth*—souls saved according to the apostolic pattern—and *qualitative growth*—

individual and corporate development according to the apostolic pattern.

Since our goal is apostolic growth, we are limited as to how much we can rely upon the growth strategies of those who are not apostolic. We can learn some helpful leadership and management principles from secular sources, and we can glean ideas from various churches. We must recognize, however, that our goals are not always the same as those of other groups. Therefore, we must carefully evaluate growth principles and methods that we obtain from nonapostolic sources and modify or discard those that do not advance apostolic goals. In the final analysis, our primary instruction in church growth must come from the Bible, from contemporary apostolic role models that have proven productive over the years, and from our own spiritual calling, anointing, and communion with God.

For example, we may hear an impressive story of a church that grew to one thousand members in two years. Before uncritically adopting the methods of that church, however, we need to evaluate its results by our goals. How many people actually attend services weekly? How many people in the church are actually filled with the Holy Spirit? Did most of the growth occur by transfer of membership from other churches? By the receiving church's own standard, were those people already saved? If so, what was the advantage to the kingdom of God? Did the receiving pastor first seek to reconcile all incoming members to their previous churches? Did he or she contact the former pastors to obtain pertinent information, insight, and recommendations? If not, in many cases the transfers will actually hinder true spiritual growth. Does the church call for biblical commitments and uphold biblical standards for leadership, or does it encourage involvement without true repentance and holiness? If so, it may give people good feelings but inhibit them from making the changes that God desires.

It is also a mistake to focus on nonbiblical strategies in an attempt to find the key to church growth. While it may be tempting to look for a new method or even a new doctrine as the key to instant revival or dramatic growth, if we want to be truly apostolic we must seek to grow by the principles of the first-century church. Methods may vary depending upon culture, location, time period, and other factors, but biblical principles remain the same.

If we truly believe that the Bible is our final authority, we will look supremely to the Bible for principles of church growth. (See II Timothy 3:16-17.) If a principle or a method is vital to church growth, then we will find it in the record of the New Testament church. If a principle or a method is not in the New Testament, then it cannot be essential.

Let us briefly discuss seven principles of apostolic revival and church growth that apply to all churches in all locations and cultures.

Prayer

The apostolic church was born in prayer. On the Day of Pentecost, the Holy Spirit fell upon 120 disciples as they waited in united prayer (Acts 1:14; 2:1). The early church maintained the habit of prayer (Acts 2:42). The first miraculous healing of the New Testament church occurred when Peter and John went to the Temple for their daily time of prayer (Acts 3:1). When the believers faced opposition and persecution, their response was to pray for boldness to witness and to see miracles take place by the power of God (Acts 4:24-31). The result of the prayer, witnessing, and miracles was spectacular church growth (Acts 4:4; 5:14).

Since God is the one who causes the church to grow, we can expect genuine growth only as we maintain a daily relationship with Him and depend upon His power to accomplish the task. The chief means of doing so is prayer. For this reason, prayer should be the first item on our agenda (I Timothy 2:1). We should maintain a constant attitude of prayer and a daily habit of prayer (Ephesians 6:18; Colossians 4:2; I Thessalonians 5:17).

We must pray specifically for (1) the *opportunity* and (2) the *ability* to proclaim the gospel effectively (Ephesians 6:19; Colossians 4:3).

Prayer is not a mechanical process whereby we earn favors from God. Rather, it is the means of communing with God and maintaining our relationship with Him. We do not purchase power from God by so many hours of prayer and so many days of fasting. Rather, prayer and fasting are the means by which we conform our minds and bodies to God's will.

In prayer, we submit to God and make His priorities our priorities (Matthew 6:9-10). Prayer does not convince a reluctant God to act on our behalf, but it gives God permission to work in our lives as He already desires. Prayer does not change God's attitude, but it changes our attitude so that we are ready to receive what God has planned for us.

In short, prayer enables us (1) *to discern God's will* and (2) *to do God's will*. Through prayer we receive the ability to live for God and work for God. When we pray in faith according to God's will, we have confidence that He will hear and answer us. (See Matthew 21:21-22; I John 5:14-15.)

Planning

By using the illustration of building a tower, Jesus taught us the importance of careful consideration, planning, and commitment (Luke 14:28). If we expect the church to grow, we must commit ourselves to growth, and such a commitment requires planning.

Jesus carefully planned for His church and prepared His disciples to lead the church according to His plan. As a man, He first prayed to obtain divine direction and then made plans accordingly. Before He chose His twelve apostles, He spent all night in prayer (Luke 6:12-13). He then took three years to train them, both by instruction and by hands-on ministerial experience.

It was God's plan for the gospel to spread from Jerusalem to the ends of the earth (Acts 1:8). As the church grew, the apostles saw the need for organization and coordination of efforts. They developed structure as needed, such as when they appointed seven deacons to assist them in administrative matters (Acts 6). Through investigations, reports, recommendations, appointments, meetings, and conferences, they facilitated church growth throughout their world. (See, for example, Acts 8:14; 11:1-4, 22-26; 13:1-3; 15:1-35; 21:17-26.)

The apostle Paul planned strategically for revival. Wherever he went, he established churches in key cities, and these churches in turn reached entire regions. He spent two years teaching in Ephesus, the capital of the Roman province of Asia, and in so doing he was able to evangelize the whole province. (See Acts 19:9-10.) To the Roman church he explained his overall strategy for ministry and then listed some concrete plans that he hoped to fulfill. (See Romans 15:19-25.) He explained his philosophy of ministry to the Ephesian elders, and to the Thessalonian church. (See Acts 20:16-38 and I Thessalonians 2.)

The apostolic church embraced the vision of the apostles, even to the extent of giving their possessions as needed for the common good (Acts 4:32-35). Church growth took place beyond Jerusalem when the entire body of believers, not just the apostles and elders, began to proclaim the message everywhere (Acts 8:4).

Persistence

We must wait patiently for the coming of the Lord, just as the farmer waits patiently for the harvest (James 5:7-8). The farmer is totally dependent upon the blessings of God—the sunshine, the rain, and the miracle of life in the seed. He cannot force growth to take place but must allow it to develop and unfold naturally. Yet he does not sit by idly and wait for God to work. He cannot do what God must do, but God will not do what he can do. Therefore, the farmer works diligently and at the same time waits patiently. The combination of diligent effort and patience is persistence.

The Christian life requires persistence (Luke 18:1; Philippians 3:14). Christian ministry also requires persistence. Despite persecution, the apostles continued to preach and teach daily in the Temple and from house to house (Acts 5:40-42). To establish the church in Ephesus, Paul held discussions in the school of Tyrannus every day for two years (Acts 19:9-10). As the New Testament repeatedly records, the apostles persevered in their ministry despite intense opposition and hardship. (See II Corinthians 4:8-13.)

Paul exhorted Timothy to work hard to fulfill his ministry—continually being watchful, enduring afflictions, and reaching for the lost (II Timothy 4:5). He compared the preacher's responsibilities to those of a soldier, an athlete, a farmer, a workman, a vessel, and a servant (II Timothy 2).

Preaching and Teaching

Preaching and teaching, together with prayer, are the most powerful means that pastors have to influence and transform people, both individually and collectively. (See II Timothy 2:24; 4:2.) Therefore, they are essential tools in establishing and growing a church.

The early church grew by the preaching and teaching of the gospel. In Acts 2, three thousand people were added to the church through the preaching of the apostle Peter, and they continued in the faith through the apostles' teaching. They "gladly received his word," and "they continued steadfastly in the apostles' doctrine" (Acts 2:41-42). Thousands more were added to the church as a result of the healing of the lame man at the Temple, but they believed on Jesus not simply because of the miracle but because of the preaching that followed the miracle (Acts 4:4).

The apostles employed preaching and teaching as the primary method of reaching souls, both in large meetings and in small groups (Acts 5:42). As the administrative responsibilities of the church grew, the apostles arranged for the selection of deacons to assist them, so that they could focus on their primary ministry, which consisted of prayer, preaching, and teaching (Acts 6:4). Paul reminded the Ephesian elders of his ministry among them, which was characterized by preaching and teaching, both in public meetings and in private homes (Acts 20:20).

The Word of God has power to change lives. When Peter preached on the Day of Pentecost, he boldly accused the crowd of killing Jesus (Acts 2:23). Instead of turning into a violent mob and seeking his own death, the people were convicted of their sins (Acts 2:37). Preaching transformed their thinking and led them to faith and repentance.

The ministry of the Word is the primary means by which people develop faith in God (Romans 10:17). Thus, to a great extent, we get what we preach and teach.

Power of the Spirit

The most important ingredient in revival is not leadership principles, management techniques, or outreach methods, but the work of the Holy Spirit. It is possible to build a strong organization and attract many members by secular principles and methods, but more than filling buildings, our goal is to grow an apostolic church—baptized in Jesus' name, filled with the Spirit, and walking in holiness. Thus, from start to finish, we must rely upon God's direction and power.

Depending on the Spirit does not mean that we can ignore all other principles of church growth. As stated earlier, we cannot do what only God can do, but God will not do what we can do. God has designed the church so that His power is necessary for growth but not sufficient in the absence of diligent effort on our part.

When Jesus gave the great commission, He specifically promised that miraculous power would accompany the preaching of the Word. The early church carried out His instructions to proclaim the gospel to everyone, and the Lord confirmed the Word with signs and wonders. (See Mark 16:15-20; Hebrews 2:3-4.)

The preaching of the apostles was accompanied by casting out of demons, speaking in tongues, divine protection from accidental harm, and divine healing of the sick. These miracles were instrumental in attracting multitudes and adding believers to the church. (See Acts 2:6; 3:11; 5:12-14; 8:6-8, 13; 14:3.)

Paul's missionary ministry was accomplished "in mighty signs and wonders, by the power of the Spirit of God" (Romans 15:19). The key to his ministerial success was not "persuasive words of human wisdom, but in demonstration of the Spirit and of power" (I Corinthians 2:4).

We need spiritual weapons, not merely human programs and methods, in order to bring down strongholds of evil. (See Ephesians 6:12; II Corinthians 10:4-5.) The strongholds are not physical locations or supernatural beings, but they are located in the human mind and personality. To overcome them, we cannot rely merely on human planning, but we must have the strategy, power, and work of the Spirit of God.

Personal Care

When the apostle Peter admonished the elders of the church, he enunciated some important principles of spiritual leadership: (1) Spiritual leaders are to serve willingly, not because they are compelled to do so. (2) They are to serve eagerly, not out of greed. (3) They are to be examples, not lording it over the church. In all these instructions, we see that leaders are supposed to care for people as a shepherd does for his sheep. They are to be good stewards of those whom God has entrusted to their care. (See I Peter 5:1-3.)

Jesus explained that leadership in the church is different from that of the world. Rather than leaders asserting authority in order to compel obedience, they serve people in order to encourage imitation of their example (Matthew 20:25-28). In short, we lead by serving others, and that service presupposes love, respect, and personal care.

Love, respect, and care for people are basic principles of Christian living, and as such they are essential to effective leadership and church growth. Jesus taught that the second-greatest commandment, right after the commandment to love God, is to love our neighbors as ourselves (Mark 12:31). He further taught that we should treat others as we ourselves wish to be treated (Matthew 7:12).

The apostle Paul provides a great example of Christian leadership and love for people (I Thessalonians 2:1-12). His personal care for them could only be compared to the combined service of both a father and a mother. He was willing to labor for them and even to give his life for them, but not to compromise truth in order to please them. He respected them so much that he would never seek to motivate them by deceit or flattery, nor would he ever take advantage of his position for personal gain or glory.

Personal Involvement

God has given the fivefold ministry to the church for the "perfecting" (KJV) or the "equipping" of the believers. The saints are equipped so that they can do "the work of ministry." Here "ministry" means "service," or all the functions of the church. Every believer should have a ministry—not necessarily public preaching but a specific place of service in the body of Christ. (See Ephesians 4:11-12.)

It is the task of church leaders to help believers find their work of ministry and train them to perform these tasks properly. In particular, those who hold the five equipping offices are to inspire, motivate, disciple, instruct, and prepare the saints so that everyone is an active, productive member of the body.

When each member performs his or her proper function, the whole body will be edified, or built up. The goal is to attain maturity in Christ (Ephesians 4:13-16). The church is like a body, a living organism. Each member has a vital role to play, although the roles are not the same (Romans 12:4-6; I Corinthians 12:4-7).

The New Testament establishes qualifications for leadership in the church, indicating that we should not rush people into positions before they are ready spiritually. (See Acts 6:3; I Timothy 3:1-13.) At the same time, Paul raised up local leaders as soon as possible (Acts 14:23).

A key to winning and retaining people is to involve them in relationships and activities. When people get involved, they get connected. They feel that they belong, they feel important, and they feel needed and wanted. Not only is personal involvement beneficial for everyone, it fulfills the biblical pattern of the members of the body ministering to one another.

The result is revival and church growth according to the apostolic pattern.

This chapter was adapted from Growing a Church: Seven Apostolic Principles *by David K. Bernard.*

LESSONS FROM OUR FOUNDERS

by Robin Johnston

Harvey Cox, Hollis Professor of Divinity at Harvard Divinity School, is perhaps best known for his book, *The Secular City*, published in 1965 in which he attempted to work out a theology for the "postreligious" age that contemporary sociologists boldly proclaimed was just around the corner. Thirty years later, in 1995, Cox made an about face with his publication of *Fire From Heaven: The Rise of Pentecostal Spirituality and the Reshaping of Religion in the Twenty-first Century*. A colleague had pushed Cox to examine an overlooked trend in the church world. This trend indicated that although mainline churches were shrinking in America, Pentecostal churches were on an unprecedented growth trajectory. Professor Cox opened *Fire From Heaven* with an admission that he, like almost all academics, had missed what could arguably be called the greatest revival in Christian history and the revival that is reshaping the face of religion in North America and around the world.

One hundred years have passed since the birth of the modern Pentecostal revival. The revival that began in inner-city missions and brush arbors has moved to fancy church buildings and worldwide organizations. The challenge of the immediate future is to resist the almost overwhelming tendency to plateau both in spiritual vigor and number of adherents. Only a deep commitment to revival can overcome the challenge. Global Impact represents the commitment of the United Pentecostal Church International to ongoing revival.

However, revival does not come just because we develop a program. Programs often help to facilitate revival. They focus our attention on the promotion of revival. But a program by itself is insufficient to bring lasting revival.

Perhaps a look back over our collective shoulders to the early Pentecostal revival will give some insight into our quest for revival. Maybe forward progress can come from a combination of revisiting the principles that created the groundswell for the early Pentecostal revival and of looking forward for innovation to face the challenges of a new century. The focus of this chapter will be on the first of the two possibilities. It will attempt a fresh look at the roots of our movement. It will highlight lessons to be learned that can help the church impact the globe.

While it is easy to see the providential hand of God in the development of the Pentecostal movement, it is also possible to trace its theological roots. God often builds upon the circumstances at hand. Historian Donald Dayton piggybacked on the rubric of Christian and Missionary Alliance founder, A. B. Simpson, to illuminate his understanding of the theological roots of Pentecostalism. Simpson understood Christ to be Savior, Sanctifier, Healer, and Coming King. Historian Bill Faupel is convinced the way to begin to understand Pentecostalism is to examine the last of these roots first. Faupel suggests that the emphasis on the second coming of Christ—and particularly the events just before Christ's return—is key.

Early Pentecostals understood themselves to be participants in the latter day outpouring of the Holy Ghost. The early church—in particular the Book of Acts church—was the recipient of the early rain. This early rain established the pattern for the apostolic church. The latter rain would restore the earlier apostolic pattern and build upon what the early church had experienced. It would go beyond the early church, not in doctrine, but in spiritual power. The latter rain was prophesied to be greater than the former rain. It would touch the four corners of the world. And then the Lord would return.

A fresh outpouring of the Spirit would herald the latter rain. A deep spiritual hunger for this outpouring was evident in the last half of the nineteenth century. Perhaps nothing captures this longing more than the following lines penned in 1883 by songwriter Daniel Whittle:

Mercy drops around us are falling,
But for the showers we plead.

And when the rain of the Holy Ghost began to fall, early Pentecostals understood it to be the promised latter rain. This understanding is evident in a number of early Pentecostal books and periodicals. Examples would be D. Wesley Myland's *The Latter Rain Covenant* published in 1910. Myland's book began as a series of articles in William Piper's famous early Pentecostal periodical, *The Latter Rain Evangel.*

This awareness of the latter rain caused early Pentecostals to be focused on missions. The gospel needed to be preached around the world before the second coming of Christ. And something supernatural was necessary to propel missions to the next level.

41

Charles Parham is considered by many to be the founder of the modern Pentecostal movement because he was the first to associate speaking in other tongues with the baptism of the Holy Ghost. There had been a number of outbreaks of tongues in the late nineteenth century. But it was Parham who took the next theological step. He insisted that speaking in tongues was the initial evidence of receiving the Holy Ghost. Parham initially understood tongues to be primarily other human languages. He thought the purpose of tongues was to prepare missionaries for work around the world. This worked on two levels. Missionaries would not have to spend months, and sometimes years, in language study. When God baptized them with His Spirit they were thought to be able to speak the language of the people to whom they were called. This also confirmed the missionaries' calling. Doubt about one's calling was removed when God miraculously gave a new language.

Parham's understanding of xenoglossic (other human languages) tongues did not last long. There were early reports where a person speaking in tongues was understood by a foreign visitor to the service. This proved to be the exception and not the rule. After a few missionaries arrived in what they thought was the land of their calling and began to speak in "tongues" and no one understood them, this idea lost its influence. However, the doctrine of tongues as initial evidence of the baptism of the Holy Ghost remained. So too did the focus on missions.

It was not without purpose that early Pentecostal worship centers were called missions. The best-known Pentecostal mission was located on Azusa Street. From that humble location, missionaries circled the globe. Some were well known like Alfred and Lillian Garr or Thomas Ball Barratt. Most labored in the shadows. Julia

Hutchins was a case in point. Hutchins is best known for her role in locking William Seymour out of the Holiness mission located at Ninth and Santa Fe because he preached the new Pentecostal message. But there is more to her story. Hutchins later had a change of heart and received her Pentecost at the Azusa Street Mission and from there carried the message to Liberia, West Africa. Hundreds of little-known missionaries like Julia Hutchins sought to carry the Pentecostal message to the four corners of the world.

The passion for missions included more than foreign lands. Early Pentecostals spread out across the United States spreading the new message. Glenn Cook left his duties as bookkeeper and general assistant at the Azusa Street Mission and traveled east to spread the revival fires. He brought the Pentecostal message to Indianapolis and Memphis. Both cities became key players in the emerging Pentecostal revival. A few years later when the "New Issue" surfaced, Cook once again headed east to spread the revelation of the mighty God in Christ.

Glenn Cook was only one of many Pentecostal pioneers who set out to spread the news that the Comforter had come. Preachers, both male and female, sometimes alone, often in groups, were intent on getting the message to the next town. They preached in hastily built brush arbors, in tents, in urban missions, on busy street corners. Sometimes they were welcomed; more often they were ridiculed; but whatever the reception, they preached on. New works sprang up across the continent. If they made a mistake it was that they frequently moved on before the new work was firmly established. So urgent was the need to get the message to the next town, they often overlooked the need to organize local churches.

As the Oneness movement emerged, it kept its missional emphasis. Evangelism was the vanguard of the church. The goal was to have everyone involved. Early Oneness pioneer S. C. McClain did not talk about the number of church members in a specific location; rather, he talked about workers. It would have been inconceivable for him to have members who were not workers. The legacy of the commitment to evangelism can be seen in the name of the headquarters building of the United Pentecostal Church International, World Evangelism Center. Evangelism and missions are to be core values of the church. In fact, one of the primary reasons for the development of an organizational structure was to help facilitate a better missions program.

Early Pentecostals understood that effective evangelism required spiritual power. They sought to echo Paul's words to the Corinthian church when he said, "And my speech and my preaching was not with enticing words of man's wisdom, but in demonstration of the Spirit and of power" (I Corinthians 2:4). The healing movement of the late nineteenth century restored the healing ministry to the church. When the Holy Ghost fell and people began to speak with new tongues, early Pentecostals began to expect the other signs mentioned in Mark 16:17-18 to follow. Nothing would catch the attention of the world like signs and wonders. Pentecostals preached faith and expected miracles.

And miracles did follow. Early periodicals are filled with miracle reports. It was not uncommon for mission halls and church buildings to have crutches and other medical devices attached to their walls as a testimony of the healing power of God. So great was this expectation that some early Pentecostals refused medical care as a sign of their faith. The more common practice was to turn to God first.

While healing was perhaps the most commonly sought miracle, early Pentecostals petitioned heaven for a vast array of miracles. They asked for financial miracles, help with relationships, and deliverance from assorted addictions. They lived in faith, trusting the compassionate nature of God. They also asked God to help them live above the power of sin. They wanted to be overcomers and they understood they needed God's help to make this possible.

Pentecostal preachers instinctively knew they needed the anointing power of the Holy Ghost to help them deliver the Word of God. Churches hungered for the fire of the Holy Ghost. Services were lively and worshipers responded enthusiastically to corporate worship and the preached Word. They wanted to experience God. They wanted their heart to feel what their head knew. Forging a personal relationship with God was more important than crafting a religious movement.

Early Pentecostals prayed until the power fell. Over the years Pentecostals have been known for powerful preaching, exuberant music, and creative worship, but early Pentecostals were best known for fervent prayer. Many a church grew out of a cottage prayer meeting. People gathered to pray and the power of God fell. Students were in a prayer meeting in Topeka, Kansas, when the Holy Ghost fell on Agnes Ozman and the modern Pentecostal movement was birthed. Crowds gathered in the Asberry home at 214 Bonnie Brae Street to pray and they incubated the Azusa Street revival. Fervent prayer brought spiritual power.

Another primary concern for the early Apostolic Faith movement was unity. William Seymour, pastor of the Azusa

Street Mission, insisted that unity was the watchword of the movement. The original intent of the movement was to bring New Testament Christianity to all churches. Early leaders initially resisted attempts to organize the movement because they did not intend to create a distinct movement. They wanted to work across denominational lines and restore the church to its apostolic roots. They wanted to move beyond denominationalism. It was only after the Pentecostal message was soundly rejected by denominational Christianity that early Pentecostals began to look at the possibility of an organization.

The impulse for unity remained in the movement, especially in the Oneness Pentecostal movement. It was woven into the fabric of the Oneness movement. In the United Pentecostal Church we often speak of "the merger" which formed our present organization. The idea of a united Oneness movement had long roots. Almost every year prior to "the merger" the idea of united movement was under discussion. A number of mergers were attempted and despite temporary setbacks the majority of the movement came together to form the United Pentecostal Church.

The early Pentecostal movement had a broad understanding of unity. It meant more than combining church congregations or organizations. It meant reaching out to all people regardless of race, gender, or economic status. Frank Bartleman famously stated, "The colorline was washed away in the blood." The Azusa Street Mission embraced all races and ethnic groups. Women played a prominent role. The revival embraced those marginalized by society. It echoed the words of Jesus when He said, "They that are whole need not a physician: but they that are sick" (Luke 5:31).

As we look back over our collective shoulders to the pioneers of this movement it is evident we can learn much from their example and sacrifice. Although prosperity has diluted our expectations, we are living in the last days. The latter rain has been poured out and it is greater than the former rain. The church must never quit being a missionary church. Too many have not heard the name of Jesus, and too many more have never been invited to a saving relationship with Him for us to rest on our laurels. Signs and wonders do proclaim His power and perhaps they can cut through the spiritual cacophony that dulls the hearts of modern people. And finally we need to passionately pursue unity so we can live out the answer to Jesus' prayer that we all might be one.

PROCLAIM THE TRUTH

by Jerry Jones

The early church was consumed with a desire to evangelize. Even before their eyes were opened to the fact that the Christian faith was more than a sect of Judaism, they spread the news of the gospel everywhere. Just as Jesus said they would, they began at Jerusalem. After the Day of Pentecost, revival spread across the city, great miracles drew crowds including those who lived in surrounding towns, and thousands were filled with the Holy Ghost and were baptized in Jesus' name. The disciples were arrested, threatened by a frightened council, released, rearrested, delivered from prison in the middle of the night, then arrested again, only to be released again. The most striking thing in the account of the Jerusalem revival was how powerless the council was to stop the revival and how utterly terrified they were of these uneducated and unsophisticated men. The Jewish leaders were simply paralyzed by their fear. It is also amazing to realize that the council was not afraid of the miracles the disciples worked, or the huge crowds that came to wherever they were. It was the preaching that they feared. Over and over the council commanded the disciples to stop the preaching and teaching: "And they called them, and commanded them not to speak at all nor teach in the name of Jesus" (Acts 4:18).

Their threats did not stop the disciples; they continued to spread the good news everywhere. The result of their fearless and faithful preaching was incredible: people were filled with the Holy Ghost and baptized every day. It may be that in a matter of weeks as many as fifty thousand were saved. What was the secret of this great revival? It was not buildings, organized effort, or structure. Their secret was simple: the frustrated council itself described it best in Acts 5:28: "Did not we straitly command you that ye should not teach in this name? and, behold, *ye have filled Jerusalem with your doctrine*, and intend to bring this man's blood upon us" (italics added). It was not personality, talent, or people skills. It was doctrine, pure and simple. The church in Jerusalem just would not quit proclaiming the doctrine, and God gave them revival.

"Ye have filled Jerusalem with your doctrine." The truth of the doctrine is the engine of revival; it is the hope of the world. Doctrine defines the church; it is what we preach, but it is much more: it is what we are. It is what makes us distinctive. To abandon doctrine is to abandon our very identity. In spite of what those who hate truth may say, doctrine properly preached and taught does not divide; it gathers people together; it turns their faces toward God. The powerful attraction embedded in truth calls to men and women in every culture and in every time.

I

Not so long ago I heard a preacher preaching from the sixth chapter of Hebrews. That happens to be a chapter that has long fascinated me, so I gave him all my attention. I was shocked and saddened by his comments on this wonderful passage. Here's what the Word of God says: "Therefore leaving the principles of the doctrine of Christ, let us go on unto perfection; not laying again the foundation of repentance from dead works, and of faith toward God, of the doctrine of baptisms, and of laying on of hands, and of resurrection of the dead, and of eternal judgment. And this will we do, if God permit" (Hebrews 6:1-3).

The preacher focused on these first three verses of the chapter, and more specifically the first verse. He taught that what the Word was urging us to do was to leave behind our immature fixation on doctrine. It served us well in the past when we were small, weak, and needed protection from the enemies' wiles. But now that we are grown up, we do not need to be so hard-nosed. All doctrine does at this point is to separate us from others from whom we could learn and who, in turn, could learn from us. So as the writer of Hebrews says, let us leave the principles of the doctrine behind us, and go on unto perfection.

What the preacher did, of course, was to pick and choose the expressions of the passage that fit his argument and ignored the rest. If we only read verse 1 up to the semicolon and stop there, the argument the preacher made that night sounds true. But the words that follow the semicolon modify the words that precede it; to ignore the words in the second half of the verse is to miss the meaning of the words in the first half.

Look carefully at the words after the semicolon: "not laying *again* the foundation." Now we clearly see the meaning of the word "leaving." It is not abandoning the doctrine, but building upon it. No building can ever be built if the foundation is constantly being dismantled and

51

re-poured. The writer is telling us to stop re-laying the foundation, but to settle it once and for all.

It has been said that it is better to debate the issue without settling it, than to settle the issue without debating it. This may be true, but to constantly debate without finally settling the issue is surely the worst result of all. Especially when it occurs within our own hearts, it is evident that constant debate is paralyzing. Hebrews 6 is a clear call to end the debate. Certainly it is a scriptural concept to put ourselves in remembrance of our faith. But there must be some foundational truths that are inviolate. Some things must finally, and for all time, be settled. These are the anchor of our souls; they are the foundation upon which all other faith rests.

As a builder pours and finishes the foundation, and then completes the building, we must pour and finish the foundation of our faith. Hebrews 6 is not a call to move from doctrine; it is a call to establish doctrine. Not laying again the foundation is the imagery not of abandonment, but of settling with certainty, then building up from there. Foundations are not made to be abandoned; they are made to be built upon.

II

This matters because the most vital part of any building is the foundation. The importance of the foundation cannot be exaggerated, since the foundation provides stability for the entire structure. The Word of God uses this imagery to teach us that our lives must have a foundation strong enough to withstand the storms of life and to provide the basis of building a greater structure to the glory of God.

What happens when there is no good foundation? Sometimes the building collapses. This is what Jesus described in Matthew 7:24-27:

Therefore whosoever heareth these sayings of mine, and doeth them, I will liken him unto a wise man, which built his house upon a rock: and the rain descended, and the floods came, and the winds blew, and beat upon that house; and it fell not: for it was founded upon a rock. And every one that heareth these sayings of mine, and doeth them not, shall be likened unto a foolish man, which built his house upon the sand: and the rain descended, and the floods came, and the winds blew, and beat upon that house; and it fell: and great was the fall of it.

The foundation was so poor that the building collapsed, and all the labor of constructing it was wasted. We have all seen those who seemed to be doing well and who appeared to be strong in the Lord, yet they suddenly collapsed in a time of stress, almost overnight. Their dramatic demise took our breath away, and made us wonder how such things could happen. The truth is they simply had no solid foundation; they had never really settled their core beliefs. They had merely gone along with the way they were brought up, or had been taught when they first came to the Lord, but had never laid the foundation solidly and firmly in their own hearts. When our core beliefs are always up for grabs, our entire lives rest on a shaky foundation.

Sometimes the collapse is not so swift or dramatic but just a slow weakening until one day the structure is beyond repair. Usually this means the foundation is weak because it does not rest on biblical truth, or perhaps it is diluted by human opinion or the demands of the present culture. Michael Pollan, in *A Place of My Own*, describes the danger of a foundation that is not solid and true:

But long before our house would collapse, the shifting of its foundation would set in motion an incremental process that would doom the building just as surely. The slightest movement of the footings would ramify throughout the structure, gradually eroding one after another of its right angles; "trueness," in the carpenter's sense, is the first casualty of a poor foundation. First the door frame falls out of square, since it is braced on only three sides. Then the windows. A building is a brittle thing, and eventually its seal against the weather will be broken—through a crack in the roof, perhaps, or in the slight discrepancy that arises between a ninety-degree window sash and what has become an eighty-nine-degree window frame. Now a drip at a time, water enters the building and the process of its decomposition begins. As Joe put it, "Pretty soon, it's termite food."

What then should be our foundation? The basis of an enduring foundation is found in Ephesians 2:20: "And are built upon the foundation of the apostles and prophets, Jesus Christ himself being the chief corner stone." The most interesting aspect of this passage is that Jesus is not the foundation; He is the chief cornerstone. The cornerstone is not part of the foundation, but rests on it.

Let me hurry to say that, of course, in one sense, Jesus is our foundation. "According to the grace of God which is given unto me, as a wise masterbuilder, I have laid the foundation, and another buildeth thereon. But let every man take heed how he buildeth thereupon. For other foundation can no man lay than that is laid, which is Jesus Christ" (I Corinthians 3:10-11).

But something else is in view in Ephesians 2. Among other things, Jesus is shown as the cornerstone because the emphasis is deliberately being placed on the apostles and prophets. This is to focus on the truth that our foundation is the Word, which God wrote through the apostles and prophets. The reason Paul was inspired to describe the "foundation" as the written Word instead of being Jesus Himself was that Paul wanted us to escape the trap the Jews fell into. The Jews did not recognize Jesus because they were looking for a Messiah who was the product of their imaginations, not the Word. You cannot build your life successfully on a Jesus of your own imagination. Our foundation is the Jesus of the Scriptures. A lot of people are in love with an idea, but not the reality. The question is whether your house is built on the Word. That determines whether it stands or falls.

The foundation for our Christian life is our "most holy faith" (Jude 20), which is the same as "the faith which was once delivered unto the saints" (Jude 3). Doctrine is not just our introduction to God; it is the basis of our continuing relationship with Him. We cannot know Him outside His revelation of Himself, and that revelation is embodied in doctrine. That means to abandon doctrine is to abandon knowing Him. The church of the Book of Acts learned this truth very early: "And they continued stedfastly in the apostles' doctrine and fellowship, and in breaking of bread, and in prayers" (Acts 2:42).

III

Doctrine is as powerful as the engine of real revival and as essential as the foundation of life for a simple reason: it is the truth. There is a power to truth; it has a life of its own. There are some characteristics of the truth that are important for us to keep at the forefront of our thinking.

The truth is absolute. That means regardless of time, situation, or circumstance, the truth is the truth. It needs no one to agree with it to be true. It needs no one to believe in it to be true. This is astonishing to us who live in a society governed by polling data. If we read that 64 percent of Americans believe something, our subconscious reaction is to believe that makes it true. But 64 percent can be wrong. What percentage of people once believed the world was flat? What percentage once believed man would never fly? Indeed, the truth is that 100 percent can be wrong. "For what if some did not believe? shall their unbelief make the faith of God without effect? God forbid: yea, let God be true, but every man a liar" (Romans 3:3-4).

The rejection of the concept of absolute truth has corrupted other fundamental aspects of logical thinking. One example is the change in the definition of the word "tolerance." *Tolerance* means "to recognize and respect the rights, beliefs, or practices of others." It does *not* mean one has to accept, or declare as right the beliefs or practices of others. If a preacher tells people they are saved without the Holy Ghost, or without being baptized in Jesus' name, I respect his right to believe that, but I do not have to agree he is correct or that the Bible backs up that teaching. Tolerance does not require me to compromise my beliefs. We love people, no matter their lifestyle, no matter what they have done. But we must continue to point them in a better direction, toward God, toward the power that enables them to choose real righteousness. We must never be rude or hurtful; we must be tolerant, but we must stand for the truth.

This wrong idea about tolerance has led to another incorrect concept about truth; that is, the idea that everyone finds his own slant on truth, and everybody is right. Look at II Peter 1:20: "Knowing this first, that no prophecy of the scripture is of any private interpretation." There is not one truth for me and another one for you. There is only one truth. Let us say someone decides it is only 50 million miles from the earth to the sun. Someone else believes it is 150 million miles to the sun. Now, they both cannot be right. In fact, they are both wrong. It is about 93 million miles. One of them is burning up, the other is frozen, and it is still 93 million miles. The truth never looks back to see who is following; it just goes on being the truth. We must conform our opinions to the Word of God. If one preacher says that you are saved by faith alone, and another says that you must be baptized to be saved, they cannot both be right. And the truth is not affected by either of their opinions.

The truth is not only absolute, it is powerful—powerful enough to set men free. "Then said Jesus to those Jews which believed on him, If ye continue in my word, then are ye my disciples indeed; and ye shall know the truth, and the truth shall make you free" (John 8:31-32). Falsehood and compromise cannot liberate; they only enslave all the more. To declare truth is to break the shackles that hold so many; it is to open the doors to the prison house. It is the only key. That is why we must proclaim truth. To do any less may gather a crowd, but it will

57

not build a church because people are not set free from sin where there is no truth proclaimed.

The truth opens the way to God. Jesus met a woman at Jacob's well in Sychar. After she realized she was speaking to a man with extraordinary insight into the things of God, she asked a question from deep in her heart: "Where can we find God? Some say Jerusalem, some say in a mountain near here, but I need to know where can I find Him?" Today many would tell her that it does not matter; God is not particular about what church or what faith you embrace; after all, all roads lead to God. That most decidedly is not what Jesus said. "But the hour cometh, and now is, when the true worshippers shall worship the Father in spirit and in truth: for the Father seeketh such to worship him. God is a Spirit: and they that worship him must worship him in spirit and in truth" (John 4:23-24). The truth is the only route to God. Not feeling, not sacrifice, not good works. Not even the presence of the Spirit, alone. There must be truth for men to find God.

Finally, truth alone will judge us. "The LORD ... cometh to judge the earth: he shall judge the world with righteousness, and the people with his truth" (Psalm 96:13). We will not be judged by earthly standards of success, but by the truth. Not by the size of our congregations, the prominence of our ministries, or the number of those who know our name. We will be judged by the truth: did we preach it, did we live it, did we love it? The only way we will make a Global Impact is to preach the truth.

> *Man with his burning soul*
> *Has but an hour of breath*

To build a ship of truth
In which his soul may sail
Sail on the sea of death
For death takes toll
Of beauty, courage, youth,
Of all but truth.

JOHN MASEFIELD

A Passion for Global Impact

by Jerry Dillon

There is no new way to have revival! What it took to get us here is what it will take to get us there. The only hope the church has to produce Global Impact is to possess the power of God's passion. God is looking for passion from His people, a passion that reflects the passion He possessed when He redeemed His people. Bible scholars often call the death, burial, and resurrection of Jesus the passion of Christ. Can you imagine a dispassionate Savior who took the job only because no one else would do it? It would be a thankless job, but He passionately accepted the role. To love the unlovable would take the life out of Him, yet He did it because He was passionate about saving the world.

Passion is far more than an action. *Webster's Dictionary* defines *passion* as "an intense, emotional, driving urge or feeling that totally possesses an individual to the point of giving oneself to a cause." People who are passionate are people who are also committed. The lethargy and lack of zeal that fills our churches today can be traced to a loss of passion. Passion is the birthplace of dreams, the impetus to all action, and the inspiration of all spiritual accomplishment.

Passion is faith's fuel. It ignites our desires while defying status quo. Passion condemns unfruitfulness. It becomes our permission to do what God has called us to do. Many men and women of God have found their permission from God because they became passionate about the things God cared about, and it loosed them into ministry. The accomplishments of the United Pentecostal Church International have been directly tied to our unbridled passion. Our future dreams and the myriad of hopes we possess will be realized only through our passion for God. Passion is the power that generates life and it is the power that moves us to perform our mission.

God Speaks the Language of Passion

What man or woman of God has ever deeply expressed his or her passion to God and found Him not understanding their words? He knows the sound of passion because He speaks the language. Consider our strength in doctrine. It comes from God's passionate commitment to His Word. God is passionate for us to know and understand Him as He really is. "Hear, O Israel: The LORD our God is one LORD" (Deuteronomy 6:4) and again, "Thou shalt have no other gods before me. Thou shalt not make unto thee any graven image, or any likeness of any thing that is in heaven above, or that is in the earth beneath, or that is in the water under the earth" (Exodus 20:3-4).

God did not want Israel to miss His master plan when He would image Himself in the man Christ Jesus. He wanted them to know that Jesus was not only their Messiah sent to save them; He was their God whom they had worshiped throughout the Old Testament.

Other utterances by the Lord let us know He is passionate about what He requires of us: "I tell you, Nay: but, except ye repent, ye shall all likewise perish" (Luke 13:3). "Jesus answered, Verily, verily, I say unto thee, Except a man be born of water and of the Spirit, he cannot enter into the kingdom of God" (John 3:5). The passion of Christ produced salvation for a world, but for that world to lay hold on salvation, they had to obey the commands of Christ as they were preached through the apostle Peter: "Repent, and be baptized every one of you in the name of Jesus Christ for the remission of sins, and ye shall receive the gift of the Holy Ghost" (Acts 2:38). The mission of the church is further realized by receiving the Holy Ghost; "But ye shall receive power, after that the Holy Ghost is come upon you: and ye shall be witnesses unto me both in Jerusalem, and in all Judaea, and in Samaria, and unto the uttermost part of the earth" (Acts 1:8). This is more than speech and rhetoric; this is the language of passion. This is the language spoken by the early church, and it must be spoken by us.

The church of Acts was born in the fires of Holy Ghost revival. Our founding fathers lived the Book of Acts and they were so possessed with passion that nothing could stop them. Even though Rome threatened and the religious rulers protested, passion allowed Peter to declare that it was better to obey God rather than men. Passion will turn fear-filled saints into fire-filled messengers. There was no river too deep, no mountain too tall, no valley too wide, or no obstacle too great that could cause them to stop preaching in the name of Jesus.

People who have passion for God cannot be stopped. You cannot kill them quickly enough, rebuke them often enough, or push them down enough to stop the strain of passion that is in them. Faith's Hall of Fame (Hebrews 11) tells of the saints of yesteryear who passionately pursued God's promises rather than choosing to enjoy the comfort that doing nothing would have offered. Some people around them might have said, "Don't upset the system. Things are fine as they are." But their passion was not listening. They would not stop because the passion in them defied the mandates of hell. You could not dampen their zeal, keep them quiet, or shut their mouths. They would not be deterred, denied, or dismayed. They simply could not be stopped. Passion is what caused the church to be the church in that day, and passion will cause the church to be the church in this last day.

The Proof Is in the Passion

Jesus proved at Calvary that passion provides the internal motivation when the external rewards drop out of sight. This is why our Lord did what He did. He endured the cross and despised the shame because of passion. His face was set like a flint to do the will of God. Passion for a lost world moved the Master to give all that He had to all that were in need. People are instructed by reason, but they are inspired by passion.

After Jesus' resurrection He showed Himself alive after His passion by many infallible proofs. My question is this, "As a church or movement, what are we after? Where do we want the church to be in twenty years?" If we want the future church to be passionate, we must first possess passion because we cannot give what we do not possess. The disciples of Jesus were passionate because Jesus showed Himself alive after the manner of His passion.

What motivates us to come to church, day in and day out? The proof that we are who we say we are will be in our passion for the message and the masses. Our mission is to connect the masses with the message. We are reconciled to God by Jesus Christ, then we are given the ministry of reconciliation. As people directly linked to the dynamic experience of Pentecost, we must be consumed with passion that carries us through the long-term plan of achieving Global Impact.

God will take passion over ability, then give you the ability to carry out His passion. Show me a man who has passion and I will show you a man God will use. I am not talking about passion as it pertains to the world around us. Many people have passion about different things. Sports fans will gather by the thousands and scream until their voices are gone. They do not mind letting you know whose side they are on. Hobbyists will rise before daylight to shop for trash and treasures in garages across our nation. But the passion I am speaking of is true passion that comes from a Holy Ghost experience with God, which changes your life, alters your mind, and renders your heart ready for service to God. Preachers, give your churches passionate messages filled with direction from above. Give them a display of passion in your life and they will reproduce it in theirs.

If we lose passion, we will become a byword to our generation. The popular word "whatever" is the antithesis of passion, and it is used prolifically today. The word "whatever" used in this fashion means, "it just doesn't matter." It seems the word "whatever" epitomizes many in our society today. Their "don't care" attitude surfaces in that one word, "whatever." It is the code word for the loss of passion! The preacher preaches about revival, and we say, "Whatever." God's requirement is prayer; our response is "whatever."

Life has a way of draining your spiritual energy. As one person said, "The problem with life is that it is so daily." Amid the daily grind, passion begins to fade. You do not lose passion in some cataclysmic event; rather, it tends to seep out until you become the shell of the man or woman you once were.

In Revelation, John commended the church at Ephesus for their discernment, their perseverance amid trials, and their work for His name's sake, but then he gave them a severe warning: "You have left your first love! You have not lost it, you've left it and if you leave something you know where it is." Hear me—it is possible to fall in love with the church and not Jesus, with the programs and not the power, with the people and not the presence.

Our prayer is that God will restore passion back into the hearts of His people. It is God's passion that energizes your life and moves you from being a spectator to a participant. Passion will turn the commands of God from legalistic drudgery to life-giving opportunities. Passion will not allow Pentecost to be your profession, but your possession. I am possessed with a passion to do more than just come to church. Church has got to come into me because He is not coming after me until He comes in me.

Who can be interested in embracing a faith that does not move the person trying to share it? If you are not moved, how can you expect anyone else to be moved? Our passion for God becomes contagious. It will not jump from the pulpit to the sinner; it must move through us to get to them.

In chapter 9 of his book, the prophet Isaiah gave a powerful prophecy concerning God's people and the way

God would bring about the great outpouring of His Spirit in the last day. In verse 3, Isaiah said, "Thou hast multiplied the nation, and not increased the joy." Is it possible to be more blessed than we have ever been and still be unhappy? We need a passion to get back the joy we once had in God. The LORD is telling His people, "I've blessed you, but why are you not happy about it?" It is not the fact that we are not growing. We are growing; we are praying new people through and baptizing new souls in Jesus' name. But the people of our churches just sit there. They have lost the joy of the harvest. We have more blessings but less joy.

"Thou hast multiplied the nation, and not increased the joy; they joy before thee according to the joy in harvest, and as men rejoice when they divide the spoil" (Isaiah 9:3). Isaiah was talking about the joy of the fruit bearer. The people who are happy are people in harvest; those who are joyful are those who are passionate about revival, harvest, and souls.

Are we trying to live our lives, do the work of the ministry, and engage our ever-changing world without passion? Without the component of passion, our frustration leads to our failure to effectively reach for our future. Someone once said that to explore, we must first excavate. To discover, we must first recover. To reframe, we must first reflect. To imagine, we must first examine. And to move forward, we must first step back. We will find our future when we go back to our beginnings. As a church, God blessed us with a strong foundation on which to build. But let us remember that we are not heritage-driven, we are future-pulled. Passion will not let us live in the land of past experience, yesterday's blessing, or Dad and Mom's prayer life. Passion opens the door to the opportunities of now!

67

How soon do we need to move concerning Global Impact? James articulated it best in his epistle: "Go to now, ye that say, To day or to morrow we will go into such a city, and continue there a year, and buy and sell, and get gain" (James 4:13). We must have a passion for now! Not tomorrow. Passion invites the Spirit of now to invade a church. Passion creates urgency that demands our response. One of our preachers was on a flight a number of years ago and he started a conversation with W. C. Firestone, the son of the founder of Firestone Corporation. The preacher asked, "What are Firestone's criteria for hiring people?" Firestone replied, "We have a simple test. The people that cannot be motivated have no place in the Firestone Corporation." People who will not be motivated have no passion to succeed in business and without passion they will ultimately fail.

In fact, passion does not operate very well in tomorrow. Passion operates best right now! Passion that is delayed, detoured, diluted, and diverted soon turns to passivity, which is defined as "the trait of remaining inactive; a lack of initiative; submission to others or to outside influences." People who do not do anything for God when they have the initial passion to do it, succumb to passivity and remain inactive because of a lack of initiative. People who have a passion to do something for God and delay doing it, often submit to the familiar voice and influence of others who say, "We've already tried that and it didn't work." Well, that was two years ago; try it again! "You can't do that in this city; it doesn't work." Do not listen to passive people because they will tell you "where it won't, when it didn't, and why it can't!" Listen to somebody that is passionate and they will tell you it can and we will! Passionate people will bring the message of Acts 2:38 to the world, and initiate Global Impact. Passion makes it happen. Thomas Edison went back to the table of invention over one thousand times before he invented the lightbulb; but he did it because he was passionate.

The pathway of passion leads to the land of accomplishment. Passion will not allow a person to remain in neutral. It consistently strives to engage the road before it and go forward. The spirit of passion refutes the idea that something should be done tomorrow and believes that everything can be accomplished now! How many churches have procrastinated in the middle of a prophecy that God gave them by saying, "When we get a bigger church, then we'll be able to start a bus ministry like the pastor across town." Or, "When we are more ethnically diverse, then I will preach against the spirit of racial prejudice." Passion screams for somebody to get up and go … now! Revival is the restoration of a passion for now! Passion will always push, pry, pull, or pick up, but it will not stop until it has succeeded in getting results as quickly as possible.

"Go to now" is the direct product of passion. The sense of urgency that we feel comes straight from the spirit of passion that Christ possessed. His word reminded disciples, "Say not there are four months and then cometh the harvest." His words compelled them to do something—now! Go to now! It is time that we go to revival; go to evangelism; go to discipleship. It is high time to awake out of sleep. Our passion will not let us sleep and be lethargic concerning the conversion of an entire world. Our passion releases God's power and moves prayer from a tedious task to a divine encounter. Our prayer, our worship, our witness will be effectively transformed because of passion. Passion pulls us into God's purpose!

In Genesis 37 Jacob's sons stood before him waiting for their next assignment. "Where will we take the flocks this time, father?" His response was, "Take them to Shechem." The word *Shechem* means "the place of burdens," and it was at the place of their father's burden that their passion for their father's purpose was tested. God often knows our passions by how we respond to His burden. They did not like it there so they left their father's purpose and the place of burdens and went to Dothan. The word *Dothan* has no meaning. God wants us to know that when we have no passion for our Father's purpose and refuse to carry His burden, we will always end up in the land of no meaning. And in the land of no meaning they said, "Let's kill the dreamer."

As a church and movement, we must not allow our dream and vision to die. I believe our passion is the strength that will bring Global Impact to the world. The world awaits eternity. May our passion provide them with God's truth and prevent them from making the wrong choice.

THE SEPARATED CHURCH

by Randy Keyes

The doctrine of separation is one of the most prominent doctrines of the entire Bible. It is difficult to distinguish the concept of the church from the doctrine of separation. The words "church" and "separation" are in some important ways interchangeable. The New Testament Greek word *ecclesia*, translated as church, means "to summon forth," to show the church as the "called out" (or separated) assembly. The church is called out not in a restricted sense, but rather we position ourselves to be blessed and receive the promises of God by coming out from the world system.

The concept of being called out goes as far back as Genesis 11 where God called Terah out from Ur of the Chaldeans to go into the land of Canaan. (See Genesis 11:31.) Terah partially obeyed, going as far as Haran. God turned to Terah's son, Abram (Abraham), calling him to fulfill what his father had left undone, namely to separate himself from family and friends and dwell in the land of Canaan. (See Genesis 12:1.) God promised Abram that he would form a new "great nation" whose people would be separated unto God.

In Genesis 13, after Abram separated himself from his nephew Lot, God again visited him with renewed promises of blessing. Although Lot had journeyed from Ur with Abram, strife between their respective herdsmen led Abram to propose that they go their separate ways. Lot chose the cities of the plain, pitching his tent toward Sodom (a symbol of corruption, immorality, and worldliness), while Abram remained apart from the cities. Immediately after they separated, God visited Abram and renewed those promises of blessings, land, and posterity to him.

Separation is even more clearly taught in God's dealings with Israel, His chosen people, especially in the record of the Exodus. Israel had suffered for generations under Egyptian bondage after the death of Joseph. Their cries of distress ascended to God, who called Moses to miraculously lead them out of Egypt to a land of their own so they could freely worship the one true living God. An analogy can be drawn in the divine way God brought them out—through the Red Sea by way of the pillar of a cloud and fire—to the New Testament church as referenced by the apostle Paul in his writings: "Our fathers were under the cloud, and all passed through the sea; and were all baptized unto Moses in the cloud and in the sea" (I Corinthians 10:1-2). The way out of Egypt (a biblical representation or "type" of sin and the world system) in the New Testament church is by our baptism in water and Spirit.

After God miraculously delivered Israel through the Red Sea, they arrived at Mount Sinai. Moses ascended to the top of the mountain to receive commandments and instructions from God as to how His people were to live and worship. The Lord's directions were detailed and specific; they affected not only their mode and place of worship, but their property rights, how they ate, their manner of dress, personal relationships, and crime. These instructions were not simply burdensome requirements and regulations; instead they positioned Israel to receive multitudes of blessings from God. God told them if they would diligently live and worship according to the law given to Moses, He would set them on high above all nations of the earth and bless every part of their lives. Consider the vast and abundant blessings promised to those who live in obedience and separation to the Lord as outlined in Deuteronomy 28:1-14.

The church, as we know it, is first mentioned in Matthew 16:18. Jesus Himself announced the beginning of the church: "Thou art Peter, and upon this rock I will build my church." While Old Testament prophets had spoken about the concept, none of them used the word "church" before Jesus did. The only possible exception is the way Stephen refered to Israel as the church in the wilderness because they were the people God called out of Egypt (Acts 7:38). The church is not called out of a nation, country, or land as Israel was called out of Egypt; instead we are called out as a distinct people. God has called us out of a life of sin and unrighteousness; He has empowered us by His Spirit to live acceptably before Him. So many today in Christianity want us to believe that separation is no longer a relevant message; however if we are part of God's church, we are a part of this called-out people, and we have separated ourselves from this world's values, customs, and ideas.

It is the intent of the enemy of our souls to spread the mistaken idea that disciplines will cause the gospel to be less attractive, and consequently, less people will desire to belong to our fellowship. The enemy would like for us to think that people do not want to be part of anything that teaches a difference in lifestyle from that of contemporary society. The enemy would try to convince us that there would be great resistance to such a message, and therefore, silence the pulpit from preaching messages about coming out and being separate from the world. If he could cause us to believe that, he will, in reality, cause us to miss out on the favor and blessing of God. The New Testament, as well as the Old Testament, is clear about the blessing and favor of God being conditional upon a life of separation.

So many honest and good ministers struggle daily with how to obtain the blessing and favor of God upon their churches. They hunger for the magnetism that draws people and seek desperately for what can be done to enhance the growth of the church. Sometimes they spend thousands of dollars and travel hundreds of miles attempting to learn a new approach to church growth or to obtain a new program that will create a revival spirit in the congregation, but often what is really missing is the clear teaching and preaching of separation.

The preaching of coming out from the world, following God, obeying His voice, and forsaking previous lifestyles and habits does not discourage people from coming to church. There is an anointing, blessing, and favor of God that comes when this message is clearly taught. There is an intensity of the Spirit, a vibrant spiritual climate that cannot be realized when worldliness prevails. The flow of the Holy Ghost cannot be present when the prevailing atmosphere of the church is worldly. There is something about a people who have truly separated themselves from this world and unto God that causes others to be drawn to believe they too can be changed and their lives made different. The doctrine of separation is not a hindrance to church growth, but rather it is the answer. I do not believe that if the church is full of world-loving people, it can experience true New Testament apostolic revival.

Many times in my years of pastoring in Modesto I have had visiting pastors ask me what is the key to great revival. I think they are expecting me to give them some kind of agenda, calendar, or outline that they can go back to their churches and follow in order to obtain the same intensity of God's power and presence. I sincerely believe the spiritual climate we enjoy has been due to my efforts to consistently teach and maintain a clear message of separation.

It troubles me when I hear people talk about our doctrine as only referring to our belief and convictions on the new birth. They call the "Acts 2:38 message" our doctrine. They call separation "holiness standards" to distinguish it from our salvation doctrine. In reality, the Bible has a whole lot more to say about the doctrine of separation than it does about the new-birth experience. This does not mean I believe less than anyone else in the necessity of the new birth, but I point this out to say that distinguishing between the salvation doctrine and holiness standards is erroneous. The word *doctrine* simply means teaching, and if so, our standards are as much a doctrine as baptism in Jesus' name and the infilling of the Holy Ghost with speaking in tongues. Our standards are not simply men's ideas and philosophies, but they are acts of separation, which again I emphasize is a prominent theme of the Bible.

Most new converts are not resistant to lifestyle changes. In my experience, new converts are so thankful for their salvation experience that they are anxious to

75

learn whatever they can do that might please God the most. If they need to dress differently, when it is explained to them appropriately, they receive it gladly. When they are taught from God's Word in such a way that they understand, they are willing to make any adjustments because they desire the blessing and favor of God. More than anything else, they want to be the recipient of His promises. Unfortunately, the resistance to separation from the world seems to come from those who have been in the church for a substantial amount of time. Over the years some have become neglectful in their prayer life and church attendance, or forgotten the pit from which they were saved, and they find themselves looking back to the things of this world and somehow these things become attractive to them. Consequently, they resist admonition to live a life that distinguishes them as the children of God. Others attack separation as nothing but legalistic, rigid, and artificial rules. However, holiness and separation have nothing to do with attaining salvation by slavishly adhering to a set of rules. We who love God want to please Him in all ways through purity of heart, thought, spirit, and lifestyle.

Let me pause here for a word on how standards should be communicated to the congregation. Many times new converts ignorantly continue to engage in their previous lifestyles and dress, and others may transfer from churches in our fellowship whose standards deviate from our own. No one should ever be threatened or publicly embarrassed, but instead they should be instructed from the Word of God in a loving, redemptive manner. "And the servant of the Lord must not strive; but be gentle unto all men, apt to teach, patient, in meekness instructing ... " (II Timothy 2:24). We should never behave as Pharisees or policemen, "neither as being lords over God's heritage, but being ensamples to the flock" (I Peter: 5:3). We do not condemn or pass harsh judgment on any brother or sister who is disobedient or weak in the matter of separation, but pray that by our loving example and patient instruction, he or she will be led to repentance and change.

The concept of holiness is a basic tenet of Scripture from the Old Testament to the New Testament. (See Leviticus 19:2; I Peter 1:15.) The seraphim Isaiah saw in his vision cried one to another about the Lord: "Holy, holy, holy, is the LORD of hosts" (Isaiah 6:3). The word for *holy* in Hebrew is *qadash*, which is translated "set apart, separated." So God, whose very nature is holy, is Himself separated from all sin, unrighteousness, and uncleanness, and commands us to follow His example. "Wherefore come out from among them, and be ye separate, saith the Lord, and touch not the unclean thing; and I will receive you ... and ye shall be my sons and daughters" (II Corinthians 6:17-18). Therefore, the foundation of our very relationship with God as His children is hindered and weakened if we do not practice holiness.

The Bible repeatedly instructs us to avoid loving the world. Jesus said to His disciples, "If the world hate you, ye know that it hated me before it hated you. If ye were of the world, the world would love his own: but because ye are not of the world, but I have chosen you out of the world, therefore the world hateth you" (John 15:18-19). The apostle John told the first-century Christians, "Love not the world, neither the things that are in the world. If any man love the world, the love of the Father is not in him" (I John 2:15).

What does the Bible mean by "the world"? For clearly, if "God so loved the world, that he gave his only begotten

Son" (John 3:16), a contradiction might seem to exist. But the Bible is not talking about the inhabitants of the world. God does not intend that we should isolate ourselves from society. We are to be the "salt of the earth" (Matthew 5:13) and "ambassadors for Christ" (II Corinthians 5:20) and "walk in wisdom toward them that are without" (Colossians 4:5). The apostle John explained what he meant by the world: "the lust of the flesh, the lust of the eyes, and the pride of life" (I John 2:16). Separation from the world, therefore, is a recognition of its lustful, prideful nature and a commitment not to participate in it, nor desire approval from it. Our actions and appearance should make clear to all who observe us that we belong to God, and it is upon His commandments that we base our lives. "Ye are our epistle ... known and read of all men" (II Corinthians 3:2).

The world is constantly trying to squeeze us into its mold and pressure us to conform to its standards, dictated by Hollywood, foreign fashion editors, music superstars, and other ungodly influences. While I understand there are some passages of Scripture that might be interpreted by one differently than another, the great majority of our standards are very clear Bible doctrines. Modest apparel is a clear doctrinal teaching: "In like manner also, that women adorn themselves in modest apparel" (I Timothy 2:9). The distinction between the apparel of a man and a woman is a very clear Bible doctrine: "The woman shall not wear that which pertaineth unto a man, neither shall a man put on a woman's garment: for all that do so are abomination unto the LORD thy God" (Deuteronomy 22:5). The fact that a woman is to have long uncut hair is a very clear Bible doctrine: "But if a woman have long hair, it is a glory to her: for her hair is given her for a covering" (I Corinthians 11:15). It saddens me that some who object so strenuously to church dress standards do not find it strange to spend time, money, and great effort to conform to the latest fad and fashion pronounced by models on a runway in Paris.

Separation also extends to our thought lives and recreational habits. In order for the old nature to stay dead—and so that sin cannot regain a foothold—we should be careful about what things we allow to enter our eyes and ears through television, music, reading material, movies, and the like. David said, "I will set no wicked thing before mine eyes" (Psalm 101:3). David had personal and painful experience with how the eye can fall on the wrong thing, causing the carnal nature to be tempted to lust, resulting in a fall into sin. (See II Samuel 11.)

Separation also extends to our social lives, friendships, and marriages. We are not to fellowship with people who are indulging in lascivious lifestyles. "Be ye not unequally yoked together with unbelievers" (II Corinthians 6:14). "Be not deceived: evil communications corrupt good manners" (I Corinthians 15:33). "Have no fellowship with the unfruitful works of darkness" (Ephesians 5:11). "Know ye not that the friendship of the world is enmity with God? whosoever therefore will be a friend of the world is the enemy of God" (James 4:4).

Indeed, separation can be summarized by this simple statement: "Abstain from all appearance of evil" (I Thessalonians 5:22).

In order for the church to have revival in these last days, we must remain a beacon of light in the darkness. We who are separated from the world, and its lusts and prideful system, are walking in light. When the world looks at us, what do they see? We cannot weaken our standards and dilute our separation or we will become part of the darkness. Let us continue to communicate the love and holy nature of God to a lost and dying world by our words, deeds, behavior, and appearance. A "light ... set on an hill cannot be hid" (Matthew 5:14).

UNITY

by Carlton Coon Sr.

Christians can be like porcupines on a cold winter night—the elements push them together, but as they get close they cannot help jabbing each other. Global Impact calls for something better. A grand unifying purpose is important. It was clearly important to Jesus.

In John 17:11-23 Jesus prayed that His disciples would be "one." He used the word "one" six times in the prayer. The repetition used by Jesus shows that it was important to Him that His followers be "one." Perhaps His repetition not only indicates the importance but the challenges involved in truly being "one."

The Unity Pattern

The first-century church lived out Jesus' prayer. The phrase *one accord* is used in the New Testament eleven times; ten of them are in the Book of Acts. Berkley translates it as *unified purpose*. Perhaps the global impact of the first-century church came through their connection to a greater cause or purpose.

Purpose enables unity. Unity does not birth purpose. Purpose births unity. A compelling purpose fuses disparate personalities.

Being in "one accord" was a defining trait of the early church, but it did not happen without challenge. In the Book of Acts, disagreements were common, as they will be in any venture involving people.

One way to begin to define biblical unity is to grasp what it is not.

Unity is not everyone sounding the same. Matthew 18:19 says, "If two of you shall agree on earth." The word *agree* is from a Greek word from which we get the word *symphonize*. A symphony is performed with diverse instruments working in unity—not unison—to create harmony.

In Global Impact's vision, one does not have to sound like the person beside him to be "on key" or to be playing the same tune. It is a symphony of agreement. Unity is not a concert of clarinets. It is not everyone sounding the same. Unity is allowing everyone to contribute his or her unique sound toward a common purpose.

Unity is not similar sensitivity. One of Paul's primary analogies for the church was that of a body. Apparently, some felt that everyone should deal with life in the same way. Paul corrected their mistaken idea.

An eye is effective for seeing. Thank God for the eye. However, cells in the eye are too sensitive to effectively grip a hammer. Eye and hand—distinct sensitivity for a distinct purpose. If all were the hand, where is the vision? If all were the eye, where is the doing? To impose similar sensitivity to every part of the body is to impair it.

In Corinth, some Christians would not eat the cheap black-market meat that had earlier been offered to idols; others did not share that sensitivity. Paul did not commend either perspective as right, but gave a balanced application to differences of opinion.

In a human body, diversity is the foundation of effectiveness. Unity is not everyone having the same sensitivity. Unity is serving toward common purpose.

Unity Is a Decision

I have decided to disconnect. This may sound strange in a chapter on unity, but you have to disconnect. John said bidding "God speed" to those in doctrinal error is to have joined in their error (II John 10-11). We choose not to be so unified.

What, then, is the basis of unity? Purpose is key, but unity is also dependent on trust. It is impossible to have a healthy relationship or collaboration without trust. People may strongly advocate for doctrines similar to those I hold, but their ethics may lead me to distrust them.

When difference and distrust overshadow purpose, unity is not possible. The chart below may give some perspective on when and where you decide to separate. Based on the target, there are dimensions of unity.

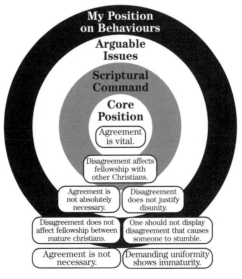

Coming together with other clergy for a high school baccalaureate service is an act of connection. The connection is temporary, and the objective is clear. The choice requires minimal agreement and nominal trust. It is unity for the moment.

Coming together with a nondenominational national group that raises money for Bibles for students is an act of unity. Again, the connection is temporary, but it is more complex because God's money is involved. Their representative comes and testifies of his experience with God. His testimony does not match up with Scripture. An offering is taken—an investment made to provide Bibles to students. Funds are sent out—there is little, if any, accountability for the funds. Doctrine is minimized for the high purpose of getting Bibles for students. It is unity for a moment and a specific purpose.

Some churches join the local chamber of commerce. It seems like a wonderful place to connect with the business people of the community. Do any members of the chamber sell alcohol in their restaurant? Perhaps an abortion clinic is also a member. Does a church's membership in the chamber of commerce serve as an approval of all the behavior of every member? Certainly not, but again a choice has been made for a different level of union and a different purpose.

To connect or disconnect is always a choice. None of us stay connected with everyone. This is not new.

- Abraham and Lot separated over their shepherds' quarrel.
- David and Jonathan separated over a king's insecurity.
- Paul and Barnabas separated over a different reaction to John Mark's failure.

- Samuel and Saul separated over Saul's egotism and lack of control.
- Diotrephes separated from John because he valued position over connection.
- Demas separated from the church because he loved this present world.

Responding to "Disunifiers"

Let me coin a new word—*disunifier*. "Unified" and "purpose" are words that go together. A *disunifier* overrides or takes precedence over the bigger purpose. Satan desires disunity in the church. He wants it to be easy to cause Christians to separate from each other. He wants the things we would separate over to be numerous and our union fragile. He prefers that the disciples not be "one." In *The Screwtape Letters*, C. S. Lewis had Screwtape (the devil) advise his nephew (Wormwood) on how to get recruits: "The church is a fertile field if you can keep them bickering." Global Impact needs a unified front.

The first disunifier is a perception of prejudicial behavior based on culture. The early church's response to this disunifier is instructive. Several years ago while preaching my way through the Book of Acts, I did some paraphrasing of the text to capture the message in my own mind. My paraphrase of Acts 6:1-3 (with apologies to those who are more proficient scholars and with no thought of my paraphrase deserving any use beyond this chapter) went like this:

As the church fellowship grew, a murmuring arose between those of different cultural backgrounds. The Greeks, generally more cosmopolitan and sophisticated than their Jewish peers, began complaining because their widows were not receiving equal treatment. In response to their complaint, the apostles gathered the disciples—of all cultural backgrounds—and told them, "This is a serious problem, but not a reason for us to leave our priorities of preaching and teaching God's Word. We cannot personally serve tables in order to make sure this responsibility is taken care of. So let's choose seven whom we know have character and integrity; full of the Holy Ghost and wisdom. We will delegate taking care of this situation and being sure the Greek widows are treated just like their Jewish counterparts.

The Grecian widows were being neglected. Should one disunify over widows being mistreated? Satan would love that. Notice the two major dynamics. The first was ethnicity and culture. It was specific. Grecian widows were the ones being neglected.

The second was consistency. Inconsistent and arbitrary treatment, whether real or imagined, becomes a problem. Church splits happen over much less significant things than what was faced in Acts 6.

The apostles aggressively responded to the concerns. Their solution had three components. It was spiritual, applied common sense, and maintained apostolic priorities.

Each man to whom the care of Grecian widows was delegated had a Greek surname. It was personal to these newly appointed deacons. They had a vested interest in those of their culture group being treated fairly.

More important than their cultural background, these men were full of the Holy Ghost, were wise, and had a good reputation. Possible cultural prejudice was responded to in an intentional way. Leaders isolated the problem and found a solution.

Lessons for Today's Church on Overcoming the Disunifier of Prejudice and Unfairness

1. Treat the problem as a real problem that will not just go away.
2. Perception is reality—if there is the perception of prejudice or unfairness, then that is at least one person's reality. It has to be addressed.
3. Keep the purpose a priority. Local evangelism and discipleship cannot be second to anything else.
4. Act intentionally. Intentionally involving the Grecian men to respond to the murmuring regarding Grecian widows was a stroke of Holy Ghost genius. God has lots of common sense! Intentionally involving any group who might otherwise be disenfranchised—like young preachers or racial and ethnic minorities—is an important step toward unity.
5. If the priority for those whom we involve in ministry is being full of the Holy Ghost, possessing wisdom, and having a good report from their peers, then do not let cultural heritage negate your priority.

The second disunifier is "I heard ... " A report came to the de facto headquarters of the early church regarding some disturbing events. "And the apostles and brethren that were in Judaea heard" (Acts 11:1) that Peter had visited a home where Gentiles lived. He had preached to them, prayed with them, baptized them, and stayed in their home.

The rumor outran Peter to Jerusalem. Put this in perspective. No current lifestyle standard would have been more significant than this concern about the Gentiles. What "they said" caused a mighty stir among the believers. Those of the circumcision met with Peter. Acts 11:5-17 is Peter's response to what they "heard."

In the apostles' response to the most significantly dis-unifying opportunity they had faced, which was based on an "I heard ... and they said," four things are evident:

1. They spoke directly with the man whose behavior was being talked about.
2. Peter's report of having received a vision was listened to and accepted as fact. Nobody else had received a similar vision. His vision led him to behave outside their comfort zone—they accepted his vision.
3. They trusted their brother, his vision, conduct, and report. Peter's testimony was accepted at face value. They did not disparage his motives.
4. Their perspective changed. Peter's explanation put them to "glorifying God" (Acts 11:18). What they had been critical of, they became joyous about.

This passage of Scripture models for us the mature behavior needed to respond to innuendo and rumor. When people want to drop "stuff" into your mind, ask if they have spoken directly with the person about whom they are talking. If not, ask if it would be permissible for you to contact the person to get clarity. Ask if their name can be used. If they have not spoken directly with the person and are unwilling to be quoted, deal with them like you would a garbage truck wanting to dump in your front yard, "Not in my mind you don't!"

An advanced model of "I heard" is when someone comes with one of those, "I'm frustrated with _____" stories. In reality, it is usually a "Will you join my cause?" conversation. When this happens, you have a responsibility to interrupt mid-sentence and say, "I think you are talking to the wrong person. You should go to the person with whom you have a difficulty and seek to resolve it in a way that saves your relationship and gives glory to the

Lord Jesus Christ." Such an action would truly be provoking one another to good works.

Lessons for Today's Church on Overcoming the Disunifier of "I Heard"

1. Speak directly to the party who is being accused. The church did not hear from those who traveled with Peter; they heard from Peter himself.
2. Trust your brother's vision, behavior, and conduct. If his vision is off, God will handle it. He can do it without human intervention.
3. Do not become so entrenched that what happens outside your comfort zone becomes something you view with disdain. Glorify God's work even when some behavior makes you uncomfortable.

The third disunifer is competitiveness. Diotrephes loved to have the preeminence (III John). His concern with John or other visiting apostles was not their message—it was the threat to his position. Diotrephes's disunifier is common. Prestige, position, and control are compelling forces. Their basis is pride.

John's remedy was to call Diotrephes's presumption what it was and promise to deal with it. Pride is the primary factor in active disunity. Proverbs 13:10 says, "pride only breeds quarrels" (NIV). Under the scab of pride, vices such as anger, rage, malice, slander, lying, gossip, and competition fester (Colossians 3:8).

Paul taught that nothing should be done for the purpose of proud exhibition. He encouraged lowliness of mind (Philippians 2:1-7). Pride sees only itself; humility sees others. Those of a Diotrephes' spirit generally infer that "it's the other guy's fault." Humility says of any problem or situation—perhaps it is my fault; time and eternity alone will prove the thing.

Intentionally replace pride with humility. A summary of Romans 12 suggests the following: Do not think of yourself more highly than you ought, but rather think of yourself soberly. Honor another above yourselves. Live in harmony with one another. Do not be proud, but be willing to associate with people of low position.

Lessons for Today's Church on Overcoming the Disunifier of Competitiveness

1. Know yourself. God uses human drives, but being keenly aware of our ambitious human nature helps keep it in check.
2. Examine yourself. What is my motive for this particular behavior or action? What is in this for me? How long since I did something without any expectation of return?
3. Apply Paul's teaching of "others first"!

The fourth disunifier is majoring in the minors. Perhaps this could best be restated as losing sight of what is important. Again consider Acts 6. The Grecian widows were not the major matter of the church. Preaching and teaching were. Satan wanted to get them to invest their energy majoring on a minor.

David Bayer wrote of a town in Tennessee with a church named "Left Foot Baptist Church." Legend has it that the name of the church referred to which foot should be washed first in footwashing. Of course, right down the highway was the "Right Foot Church"!

The Lesson for Today's Church on Overcoming the Disunifier of Majoring in the Minors

1. Is your community being aggressively evangelized? Did every first time visitor get a follow-up contact last week?
2. How many Home Bible Studies are being taught?
3. Does the congregation reflect the cultural diversity of the community?
4. How many were converted last year?
5. How many graduated from a discipleship class and are now involved in an active role of ministry?

Unity Is a Verb!

Unity is never inactive. In *Mastering Outreach and Evangelism*, authors Ratz, Tillapaugh, and Augsburger note, "In war there is only one objective on the front line: defeat the enemy. Everyone pulls together; there's no time to complain. But when you get a few miles behind the front line, everyone is complaining about the food, the mail, the weather. When you leave the front line, griping becomes a way of life." Prejudice and preference are set aside at the front line of spiritual battle.

One of the growing ministries of the Home Missions Division is the *Church-in-a-Day* (CIAD) program. A CIAD project builds a new church building for a young church. The building goes from a bare slab to a finished building in twenty-four hours. It is a wonderful thing to witness.

There has been an interesting by-product of the ministry. Two hundred workers come together for a CIAD. Pastors who could barely stand to speak to each other—having labeled each other and fussed over saints that moved—are

91

suddenly sweating together on the same project. There is common purpose. Several have spent part of their CIAD project in tears, repenting of past pettiness. When you take hold of something bigger than you are it takes hold of you.

In two passages (Matthew 5:23-24; 18:15-17) Jesus taught the proper procedure for dealing with problems. If your brother offends you, go tell your neighbor? Your presbyter? No! You go to him alone; sit down with him and say, "Here's a problem I want to resolve." If that does not resolve it, then Jesus instructed one to involve other people. The final court for unresolved conflict was the church. Apparently, it was Jesus' expectation that the decision of the body would be respected. The Bible said that in working out our differences, we win our brother.

When one is out of sorts—not if, but when—there is a Christian responsibility to take the high road of conflict resolution. The problem is usually in our tongue. Maturity demands that we bite our tongue to keep from saying in a private conversation with an uninvolved person that which we have not confronted in private dialogue with a specific person.

A Covenant of Ministerial Unity

Perhaps we need a covenant to help us. In the late 1940s, four men, including Billy Graham, met outside Modesto, California. Billy Graham directed each man to pray about their future ministry. When the four came back together they listed four problems that were hindering their evangelistic efforts.

Facts were commonly misrepresented by itinerant evangelists. Evangelists exaggerated the size of crowds, the number of converts, and the financial need. Each man pledged to report accurate statistics.

Financial accountability was a problem. Because evangelists aggressively raised money to pay their expenses, it appeared many were in it for the money. The four decided their financial books would be open and that their personal salary would not reflect the offerings in a crusade.

Moral misconduct was a problem. They committed to never being alone with a member of the opposite sex.

Itinerant preachers were commonly critical of efforts of pastors in an area in which they ministered. The four men committed to a positive ministry; they would never speak disparagingly of any pastor.

Their response to those four problems became the basis of what is known as *The Modesto Manifesto.*

Since Satan would use every possible disunifier to affect our unified purpose, the Global Impact initiative calls for a similar decision. A call to action, a manifesto of unity. Maybe the best way to begin the Global Impact initiative is to have each minister sign a covenant of ministerial unity. I have already signed one. It is time for radical action. A spirit of collaboration is awakening. Global Impact does not leave out any aspect of this great work.

Covenant of Ministerial Unity

1. I will practice with my ministerial peers the level of respect, honor, and trust that I would expect from any mature saint.
2. I covenant to maintain a Matthew 18 relationship with every fellow minister. Christ requires that I take any problem or concern to that specific person.
3. I covenant to actively practice doing unto others what I would want them to do if I were in exactly the

same situation.

4. I will not attach a label to anyone. Unless I have sat in his or her congregation, heard him teach, and observed her daily conduct, I do not know where he stands on most things.

5. I commit to trusting my brother or sister. I trust they are hearing from God even as I attempt to do the same.

6. I will assume the best rather than the worst. Any information—news or gossip—will not be believed or repeated until I have spoken directly with the person involved. Gossip is an activity of the immature. The less I know and repeat about other people's affairs, the more attention I can give to God.

7. I will control my tongue. I have decided never to speak ill of another minister to any saint in any church. I will not foster a spirit of contempt or competition.

8. I empower others to rebuke me if I begin to speak ill of someone who is not there to defend himself or herself.

9. I accept the responsibility of rebuking another brother or sister who speaks ill of one who is not present to defend himself or herself.

10. I covenant to deal with controversy and disagreement in a way that keeps the unity of the spirit.

11. I make a decision to submit to authority. I will not always agree with authority, or with every decision of every conference, committee, or board. However, I have decided to submit.

12. When I disagree and can no longer in good conscience remain in fellowship, I will disconnect in the right way, with the right spirit and right actions.

_____   _____

Name   Date

Global Impact through the Supernatural

by Bruce A. Howell

One, two, three, four, five, six, seven, eight, nine, ten... days represented the count-up of focused prayer preceding the launching of the New Testament church. Pentecost fully came. Blast off! The Spirit is still empowering the church as we take the gospel around the globe (Luke 24:49; Acts 1:8). "And they went forth, and preached every where, the Lord working with them, and confirming the word with signs following. Amen" (Mark 16:20).

We often study the Book of Acts, but do we practice it? School is out. Quit studying the course. Start running with it! We, in the Foreign Missions Division, have established our theme and working mode of operation as, "I have set before you an open door" (Revelation 3:8, *NKJV*). Doors are opening faster than we can sprint through them. His Spirit is in us, enabling us, energizing us, and working through us. He beckons, "Go, church, go!" He promises, "I will be with you!" What a scene of mind-boggling potential—our unlimited God working hand in hand with limited man.

The God of Global Impact

Some briskly read the twenty-eight chapters of Acts, thinking it represents a few days in the life of the early church rather than thirty-plus years of history. It is not uncommon for a person to nostalgically confess, "Oh, if I could only live in the days of Acts!" Personally, I am quite content to be alive in the twenty-first century. The Acts of the Apostles continued with "all that Jesus began both to do and teach" (Acts 1:1). The church today has this "same Jesus" (Acts 1:11; Hebrews 13:8). Retired missionary, Nona Freeman, stated, "The Word is a time-proven irrefutable fact. Whatever God has done through the ages, He can do it again, and more, much more than our finite minds can comprehend. ... Name the need, and He can and will do it. ... His limitless power will do whatever we believe Him for. No exceptions. ... In our forty-one years in Africa ... we saw every miracle recorded in the Book of Acts happen in our services."

I will mention three of the many unalterable things about our never-changing God. Anything He has ever done before, He wants to do today. Anything He is doing anywhere else in the world, He wants to do where you are. Anything He has ever done for anybody else, He is ready to do for you.

Alex Marquez Sr. was preaching in a small Mexican town. He told the story of blind Bartimaeus. (See Mark 10:46-52). A man, whose blind brother was in the service, began to cry, "If God could do it then, can He do it now?" He took his blind brother by the hand and led him to the front. He asked, "Preacher, do you believe my brother can be healed?" With simple faith Brother Marquez affirmed that God could and would heal. He laid hands on the man who instantly began to shout, "I can see! I can see!" The church exploded in worship. The people were amazed. This man had lost his sight eighteen years earlier when his eyes were gouged from their sockets during a fight.

At three o'clock in the morning of the next day, Brother Marquez was awakened and summoned to the town plaza. Over fifty people were waiting to be baptized in Jesus' name. The healed man had gone around the neighborhood testifying of what God had done. Nothing attracts attention and brings people running like a church on fire and miracles happening.

The Church of Global Impact

General Superintendent Kenneth F. Haney said, "As a church, we will never influence and capture the attention of the world without the supernatural power of God." I am not talking about emphasizing miracles and minimizing doctrine. We constantly need a truth encounter (clear explanation of the plan of salvation) and a power encounter (clear demonstration of God's Spirit and power). It is not either/or. It is both.

In 2006 in the overseas works of the UPCI, 110,278 received the baptism of the Holy Ghost and 91,671 were baptized in the saving name of Jesus Christ. Allow me to speak of things I have seen and heard. I was privileged to preach a crusade in Pakistan, a nation of 162 million people. The first night I spoke on healing. At the closing I prayed the prayer of faith. At that moment, a Muslim driver of one of the rented buses came into the arena to see if his passengers were ready. This man had a grapefruit-sized tumor in his stomach. As he drove the bus later that night, he felt the tumor dissolving. The next night he came and testified in front of seventeen thousand people that Jesus had healed him.

During the service, many written prayer requests were brought to the pulpit. One was for a lady lying in a coma in a hospital 250 miles away. We learned later that at the exact time prayer was made, this lady opened her eyes, sat up and shortly after, left the hospital, totally healed. In that crusade we estimated that one thousand people received the Holy Ghost.

When Sister Howell and I first arrived in El Salvador our conventions were held in a small gymnasium with three to four thousand in attendance. As the church grew, we moved to the National Gymnasium and had twenty thousand in attendance. I often passed the largest sports stadium in El Salvador, and would tell North American visitors, "One day we will have our national convention there." A few years ago, I returned to preach the national convention in El Salvador at the Cuscatlan Stadium. My dream had come true. Over thirty seven thousand people were in attendance.

Here in North America, a missionary just concluding a year of deputation saw 4,400 people receiving the baptism of the Holy Ghost and over 1,600 baptized in Jesus' name during his travels. At the general conference in Tampa, 587 were filled with the Holy Ghost.

You and Global Impact

I have noticed nine "be-attitudes" of those longing to be used in the supernatural. I am sure there are more. These are illustrated through Scripture and supernatural stories.

Be Available: God is looking for someone accessible, a vessel ready to be used. In our services, when the Spirit begins to move, business as usual is tossed aside, and we follow the leading of the Holy Ghost.

Vic Votaw, regional evangelist to Asia: During hospital visitation, I was told a sixteen-year-old Chinese girl was dying. I went in, introduced myself, and asked to pray for her. She requested a Christian song in Chinese. As I sang, "As the Deer," she wept, telling me that at fourteen she was abandoned by her parents and forced to live on the street and later became a prostitute. After I went home, the hospital called to say she had checked out and that it was dangerous since she was on kidney dialysis four days a week. That same day, she came to my house and told me while she was singing the song I had taught her, the Lord healed her. She wanted me to baptize her in Jesus' name. I gladly obliged, and she received the Holy Ghost, becoming one of our precious believers in Taiwan.

Be Empowered: We must go beyond the natural—what we can do—to the supernatural—what God can do—in order to reach our generation. Planning and administration are necessary parts of what we do. But the salvation and deliverance of lost souls is our ultimate goal. It represents the greatest miracle of all and is our only reason for existence. Many are in bondage and addiction. To enter the strong man's terrain and take back our possessions requires a stronger authority. We possess the power. It is still in the name of Jesus. We must go beyond mere skills acquired in psychology classes and counseling courses. I do not discredit these. They have their place, but we need divine intervention. God desires not only to inform minds, but to transform hearts.

99

Be Expectant: Come to church expecting God to move. Go to the pulpit desperate for a demonstration of His power. The problem with hit-and-miss preaching is that it usually does just that: hits and misses. Be results-oriented. Have an objective in mind. God's Word never returns void (Isaiah 55:11). It accomplishes its purpose: to chastise, convict, challenge, and change.

Billy Cole talked for years of a day coming when thousands would receive the Holy Ghost in a single service. It has happened, is happening, and will continue to happen. He once stated we could see a drastic increase in the supernatural. When asked how, he explained, "Preach it more! You get what you preach."

Our mandate remains, "The Spirit of the Lord is upon me, because he hath anointed me to preach the gospel to the poor; he hath sent me to heal the brokenhearted, to preach deliverance to the captives, and recovering of sight to the blind, to set at liberty them that are bruised, to preach the acceptable year of the Lord" (Luke 4:18-19). Believe that it can happen, will happen, and it does. Preach it. Equip the saints to do the work of the ministry (Ephesians 4:12). A catalyst for the miraculous is the simple faith of believers. "And these signs shall follow them that believe" (Mark 16:17). We enter the sanctuary to worship. We leave stepping into a sin-stricken and troubled world. Problems abound, but God's power much more abounds. Divine appointments and opportunities await.

Be Bold: Peter said, "Look on us" (Acts 3:4). Boldness grabs attention. "Grant unto thy servants, that with all boldness they may speak thy word, by stretching forth thine hand to heal; and that signs and wonders may be done by the name of thy holy child Jesus. ... and they spake the word of God with boldness" (Acts 4:29-31).

Antonio Marquez, missionary to Costa Rica: Alexis, a darling seven-year-old missionary kid, was called to the platform recently by Brother David Hudson in Morgantown, West Virginia. He explained what happened the night before. A little girl was sitting next to Alexis in service. As Brother Antonio Marquez made the call for people needing the Holy Ghost, Lexy asked the girl if she had received the Holy Ghost. The little girl responded, "No, I'm scared." Alexis retorted, "Shame on you! The Holy Ghost is nothing to be afraid of. It is the Spirit of God living in your heart." She then commanded, "Raise your hands. I am going to lay hands on you, and you are going to speak in other tongues as God fills you with the Holy Ghost." When Lexy laid hands on the girl, she started speaking in tongues! Oh, for child-like faith, and matching boldness.

Be Humble: Pride causes the conduit of the supernatural to cease in our lives. The same man who boldly proclaimed, "Look on us" later pleaded, "Don't look on us! Look to God" (Acts 3:12).

Be Faithful: I want to be full of faith. Faith's definition has not changed. It is still "the substance of things hoped for, the evidence of things not seen" (Hebrews 11:1). Without faith it is impossible to please God (Hebrews 11:6). We walk by faith, not sight (II Corinthians 5:7).

Be Sensitive/Perceptive: Have a listening ear and an open heart. "And there sat a certain man ... being a cripple from his mother's womb, who never had walked: the same heard Paul speak: who stedfastly beholding him, and perceiving that he had faith to be healed, said with a loud voice, Stand upright on thy feet. And he leaped and walked" (Acts 14: 8-10).

Eugene Dominguez, AIMer to Peru: One night, in a recent crusade, we were praying for people in the crowd when I noticed a young teen that appeared crippled. I started to pray for him and he became afraid. So I did not lay hands on him. The boy was carried into the building again the following evening. As the preacher concluded his message, I approached the boy and his mother. I asked her what she wanted God to do. She said, "I want my boy to walk." As we prayed for him in the name of Jesus we helped him to take a step. He then took a step by himself, then another, and another. A big smile appeared. He walked freely around the coliseum. This notable miracle was a turning point in the crusade with hundreds receiving the Holy Ghost that night and the night following.

Be Obedient: When the Spirit speaks, obey. "Whatsoever he saith unto you, do it" (John 2:5).

Tim Olson, missionary to Scandinavia: John Schumacher had visited our church several times. This elderly man was born a Catholic and he was going to die a Catholic (or so he told his two daughters who attended our church). But, as is often the case, when John discovered that he had stomach cancer, he called his tongue-talking daughters and asked for prayer.

The situation was serious. A small group of about fifteen people drove over three hours to the hospital in Ashley, North Dakota, to pray for John. As we walked into the hospital, I felt prompted by the Holy Ghost to ask the nursing staff if we could have a chapel service. They eagerly made a room available and brought the sick and elderly for the service. At least fifty gathered.

Staring me in the face was the most unusual collection of people that I ever witnessed in one church service. Wheelchairs and walkers were everywhere and even a hospital bed could be spotted here and there around the room. The start was a bit awkward but when we sang "Amazing Grace" the atmosphere was transformed. Tears welled in people's eyes and slid down their cheeks as the sweet presence of the Savior became evident.

The message that night was simple and the concluding prayer was nothing memorable but everyone knew that God had met us. This was not your normal Pentecostal church service. It was just a small group of people in desperate need of God's touch. And touch us He did!

The next day doctors performed a MRI on John and the results contradicted what the earlier tests had conclusively revealed. The doctors were perplexed. The cancer was gone. This irrefutable medical proof convinced John, his wife, a daughter and two sons and their families that Pentecost was real. They were all baptized in Jesus' name and all of them received the baptism of the Holy Ghost. The died-in-the-wool Catholic John Schumacher went everywhere in Ashley telling people what God had done for him. John so badly wanted to let others know about supernatural power that when an old Methodist Church building came available he bought it. Today, in Ashley, North Dakota, the First United Pentecostal Church stands as a testimony to the miraculous power of God.

Be Confident in the Lord: "Then Peter said, Silver and gold have I none; but such as I have give I thee: in the name of Jesus Christ of Nazareth rise up and walk" (Acts 3:6). Our services need to be filled with praise and worship, which usher in the presence and power of God. We create an atmosphere where God can work. Magnifying God unveils His greatness compared to our littleness. He is greater than all our situations and wants to work on our behalf. "Praise him for his mighty acts: praise him according to his excellent greatness" (Psalm 150:2).

John Hemus, missionary to the United Kingdom: Our son Matthew called and told us he had numbness in his hands and feet. We were in the States at the time and my wife was about to return to England. Within two days our son was paralyzed from head to toe, diagnosed with "Guillain Barré Syndrome."

While in prayer for Matthew, I was transported to the hospital ward where he was lying. I stood at the foot of his bed, observing him and the room around him. I watched a man walk up to him and look at me. He leaned toward Matthew and touched his body. As He did, he looked at me and said, "It has stopped and he will now recover."

I called my wife in the morning and asked about Matthew. She responded, "I feel it has stopped and he will recover." I asked why she said that and she explained while she was praying that morning that is what she felt. I inquired where she was standing. She was at the foot of his bed. I told her what was in the room, where the window was, and the cabinet and other things. She said, "How on earth do you know that?" I had stood there the night before! In two days I flew to England to see my son. I walked into the room I had supernaturally stood in the week before. Matthew pulled up his legs, slid off the bed, and stood before me. The doctor confessed, "This is remarkable. This is incredible." I responded, "No, Doc, this is a miracle!"

Be Persistent: Sometimes, we give up too easily. Keep believing. God is able (Ephesians 3:20).

Philip Tolstad, missionary to Uganda: A little girl was terminally sick in Malawi, Africa. The local Pentecostal ladies decided they would go and pray. Her dad was a witch doctor but agreed that they could pray for his daughter. They removed the charms, prayed for her, and left. Later, information came that the girl died. One lady refused to give up. When she heard the news, she got up, and rushed back. She shouted over the dead body, "In the name of Jesus, get up!" What happened? The little girl got up. Persistence paid off!

I am ready to put this down, jump up, rush out and lay hands on the first person I meet with a need. How about you? If so, here is one more supernatural story for the road.

Dr. Doris Jungco Fuller, Philippines: November 7 is always special to me. It is the day I received an urgent call to the intensive care unit. My little eight-year-old nephew was involved in a car accident. At the ICU, the sight of my nephew left me speechless. I hardly recognized him. His face was markedly swollen, bluish to black in color. His eyes were shut from the swelling and there was blood oozing from his ears. The boy's father was also a medical doctor. Diagnosis revealed three skull fractures, broken ribs, and worst of all, a cerebral hematoma. My nephew was being scheduled for a craniotomy, a life-threatening surgical procedure where a hole is made through the skull in order to reach the source of bleeding and evacuate the clotted blood. This process is like a double-edged sword that could save a patient's life, but could also cause serious and undesirable effects.

The question was: "Should I tell my family what I knew and believed; that there is a Doctor who is greater than any human doctor, and that in the church where I attend, I have seen sick people healed by the power of His name? Should I risk another round of insults and accusation of being a disgrace to our family?" Suddenly, I felt a surge within me and I said to myself, "Now or never!"

Outside the ICU, I asked my brother, "How much do you trust human doctors?" Here we were, two medical doctors, considering a question that shakes the very foundation of what we represent professionally. To my amazement, he looked down without speaking a word, shook his head, and tears began to form in his eyes. Without planning on my part, words started flowing that had been suppressed for a long time. "There is a Doctor who is greater than any human doctor. His name is Jesus! He is our only hope now. For the sake of your son let's have him prayed over by my pastor immediately." I must have uttered those words with so much conviction that, without any question, he said, "If you believe so, then let it be." All the family members present in the hospital that after-

noon agreed to have my pastor come and pray. For the very first time, a man of God was warmly welcomed by most—if not all—of my family, and allowed to minister. The Lord touched and miraculously healed my nephew that night. The operation was cancelled. There are no deformities as a result of that accident, not even a scar to show for it. The doctors declared what I already knew: my nephew's case was a "miracle."

My parents forgave me for "abandoning" our family and becoming Pentecostal. My mother was baptized in Jesus' name forty-five days before she died. My sister-in-law, another brother, and his son were also baptized and received the Holy Ghost. Thank God I realized there's a greater doctor in the house!

I will race you to the open door. Step through to fresh opportunities in making a Global Impact through the supernatural.

THE FINAL THRUST

by Paul Mooney

The challenge embraced by the United Pentecostal Church to conduct a new "Global Impact" in terms of revival and evangelism demands sacrifice and commitment. If we think of it in relationship to the last days we will see it as perhaps a "final thrust." The commitment begins with a Holy Ghost inspired one-mindedness reminiscent of our apostolic fathers. In this chapter, let us consider that basic point, "being of one mind." When a passionate and anointed message of salvation and revival is proclaimed, and yet there are those who categorically dismiss it as irrelevant while they walk away unaffected, uninspired, unconvinced, and unburdened ... what are they thinking? The apostle Paul asked a similar question: "Am I therefore become your enemy, because I tell you the truth?" (Galatians 4:16). What sort of mind-set governs such responses?

Before we can accept the challenge of a coordinated final thrust of global evangelism, we must first allow it to be birthed in our hearts and our minds by the Holy Spirit. The Bible says that as a man "thinketh in his heart, so is he" (Proverbs 23:7). What we think in our hearts may well determine what we accomplish.

Paul's challenge to us and to the Philippians to "let this mind be in you, which was also in Christ Jesus"

(Philippians 2:5) may not be an easy thing to understand in its full meaning, but surely it suggests that we are to be like Jesus, to think like Jesus. If we have the "mind of Christ," we will believe and act upon the principles and definitions that Jesus gives us. We will claim as our own the same thoughts, conceptions, and ideas. Consider a couple of the powerful concepts given to men by Jesus: "Lift up your eyes, and look on the fields; for they are white already to harvest" (John 4:35). "And I, if I be lifted up from the earth, will draw all men unto me" (John 12:32). If we have the same mind as Christ, these ideas will be reflected in our behavior and our beliefs.

The philosophers say that a person may know what he himself thinks but cannot know what anyone else thinks. We can see that others are physical creatures, but how can we be sure they have a mind? And if we assume they do, we still do not know what sort of thoughts they have. It is along these lines that the battle over human consciousness rages. Nuances and complex arguments aside, the final word about human consciousness is widely believed to be expressed in one's behavior. Think of it this way: if someone has a similar response as you (such as the same reaction to painful stimuli as you yourself have experienced) then it holds that the other person's mind is thereby acknowledged and must be similar to your own, based on common reactions. In other words, if the physical response of two people is the same, then we may conclude they are thinking alike.

Most of us have probably observed at one time or another that others in our lives do not think as we do. Most likely we base this perception on their behavior or their responses to situations. We may even ask, "What in the world were they thinking?" This notion can apply to our behavior as it relates to obedience to the Word of God or in response to the call to prayer and revival.

These are troublesome times, but nothing about the true Christian mind need be negative. We may be forced to fight battles and wage war against false doctrine, but never in hopelessness. Through faith we are assured that truth will triumph. Let this "mind" be in you: walk up your mountain, carry your cross, believe, go forth, give, bury your fears, destroy your resentments, live in faith, walk in faith, love your enemies, preach the Word, be instant in season and out of season. And shout with a voice of triumph.

If we possess the "mind of Christ" it will be reflected in our behavior. We will become men and women of like faith, dwelling together in unity. (See II Peter 1:1, Psalm 133:1.)

The matter of living in the last days does not suggest retreat or drawing back, but rather demands a new effort, a final thrust of world evangelism. It demands renewed consecration, an encompassing vision, and a sure word of prophecy. It demands not less of us, but more—more effort, more giving, more faith.

THE MASTER PLAN

by Jack Cunningham

In the long run men hit only what they aim at.
–Henry David Thoreau

Vision takes a purpose and starts to turn it into specifics—what specifically we will do, when we will do it, and how we will accomplish it.

In late 2006, General Superintendent Kenneth F. Haney gathered a group of pastors and leaders to share his vision for doubling the United Pentecostal Church International in ten years. In the following months, extensive plans were developed, leaders appointed, timetables set, and promotional materials produced. Global Impact was unveiled and enthusiastically received during General Conference in Tampa, Florida. In a nutshell, Global Impact is a grassroots initiative designed to double every aspect of the United Pentecostal Church—from the local church to the international body.

The fulfillment of this vision is the very essence of the responsibility of the church—which is, to reach every culture, race, and religion with the gospel.

Global Impact is a ten-year growth initiative, which began in January 2008 and will continue through December 2018. In order to double in ten years an average net growth rate of approximately 7.2 percent must be reached.

Kenneth Haney has challenged every local church, section, district, division, and the international body to set goals for doubling every trackable program, event, data source, category, offering, and so forth. One of the keys to the success of this endeavor is to diligently and accurately track and measure our progress.

The Focus of Global Impact

The first time I met with Bishop Haney to discuss Global Impact, he brought with him a yellow legal pad with literally pages of handwritten notes. One of those pages contained a listing of the basic goals he hoped to accomplish through Global Impact:

1. Double the United Pentecostal Church International in one decade!
2. Focus the North American and International church on evangelizing the world with the Acts 2:38 message.
3. Involve the total church. His goal, many times reiterated, is that every member and minister, from the local church to the international body, would become involved with Global Impact.
4. Fulfill the destiny of the end-time Apostolic church by impacting the world for Jesus Christ.
5. Re-indoctrinate every member of the United Pentecostal Church with the message of salvation, gifts of the Spirit, evangelism, holiness, separation, and the Godhead.

Simple, Participatory, and Measurable

Determine that the thing can and shall be done and then we shall find the way.

–President Abraham Lincoln

114

Successful programs, those that reach maximum effectiveness, encompass three essential elements—the program is simple, participatory, and measurable.

Simple—The program must be easy to understand and easy to implement. Global Impact is a ten-year initiative that seeks to reach an attainable growth goal of 7.2 percent per year. Henry Ford said, "Nothing is particularly hard if you divide it into small jobs."

Participatory—The program must involve a maximum number of participants. Global Impact will seek active participation from every local church and pastor, from leaders at the district and national levels, as well as from missionaries and national leaders worldwide. Thus, Global Impact is a "grassroots" growth initiative.

Measurable—The progress of the initiative must be easily trackable. The goal of 7.2 percent annual net increase over one decade is easily measurable. Every local church is asked to track the number that are water and Spirit-baptized annually, as well as its Easter Sunday school attendance. Every district is asked to track its number of ministers and churches. Every division, operating at World Evangelism Center, is asked to track programs, participants, registrants, events, and fundraising.

Passion to Reach the World

One of the many powerful and distinctive traits of the ministry of our present general superintendent is his ability to communicate his passion to reach the lost. He has made it crystal clear to us that he believes the United Pentecostal Church International should be the most powerful evangelistic force in the world. On more than one occasion Bishop Haney told the committee,

"Only a passion to reach the world with this message will keep this organization viable and distinct!"

Global Impact Resources

Web Site—An attractive and easy-to-use Global Impact Web site has been established and is in operation. The address is *www.GlobalImpactUPCI.com*. When you log on you will find up-to-date information, downloadable files and artwork, and much more. For more information you can contact the webmaster, Doug Joseph, at *CACPstr@aol.com*.

District Global Impact Director—General Superintendent Haney has requested that every district superintendent appoint a district Global Impact director. At the time of this writing all fifty-six districts in North America have a Global Impact director.

The district Global Impact director's responsibilities include the following:

1. Promote Global Impact within the district.
2. Assist the district and local church in setting goals.
3. Gather trackable information.
4. Maintain accurate records.
5. Report information to Global Impact.

The district Global Impact director, working closely with his district superintendent, will aggressively promote Global Impact at annual district events. He is available to assist pastors and churches with Global Impact.

Pastors, Leaders, and Members Action Plan— Two passport-type workbooks have been designed and distributed to all pastors to assist them with strategic planning for their local congregation's involvement in Global Impact. These passports are available free of charge. To order, contact Ed Snyder at *VaDistAdAsst@aol.com.*

DVD—A short introduction of Global Impact by the general superintendent is available in DVD format. This presentation would be great to use to invite your church to participate in Global Impact.

Global Impact Structure

Planning, details, and action steps have all been put in place designed to more effectively bring this vision to fruition. One of the action steps was to put together a far-reaching structure to serve as a vehicle for getting Global Impact to every facet of the fellowship. It has been said of many failed programs, "People don't plan to fail—they fail to plan." With that in mind the general superintendent, with the endorsement of the general board, has created the following structure to carry out plans for Global Impact:

Step one: Appoint a Global Impact director.

Step two: The Global Impact director, with the endorsement of the general superintendent, appoints the Global Impact steering committee.

Step three: The general superintendent appoints a Global Impact subcommittee of the general board made up of all district superintendents.

Step four: The Global Impact director, with the endorsement of the general superintendent, will appoint subcommittees to carry out various responsibilities.

Foreign missions: In addition to the above North American church structure, the Foreign Missions Division has put in place a structure for planning, implementing, and promoting Global Impact throughout the world. The structure begins with the General director of Foreign Missions, and includes regional directors, appointed foreign missionaries, and field superintendents.

Goals: Ministers and Churches

Set your goals. Tend to your goals. For he who aims at nothing is sure to hit it.

The Church Division provided the following statistics for the North American Church:
- Number of credentialed ministers:
  January 2008: 9121.
- Global Impact Goal—Number of credentialed ministers:
  December 2018: 18,242.
- Number of local churches:
  January 2008: 4143
  - Canada: 225
  - United States: 3918
- Global Impact Goal—Number of churches:
  December 2018: 8286.
- Number of daughter works:
  January 2008: 290.
  - Canada: 14
  - United States: 276
- Global Impact Goal—Number of daughter works:
  December 2018: 580.

The Foreign Missions Division provided the following statistics for fields where we have a United Pentecostal Church presence outside of North America:
- Number of credentialed ministers:
  January 2007: 17,214

- Global Impact Goal—Number of credentialed ministers:
  December 2017: 34,428.
- Number of local churches and preaching points:
  January 2007: 23,298.
- Global Impact Goal—Number of churches and preaching points:
  December 2017: 46,596.

The General Sunday School Division provided the following statistics for the North American Church:

- Number of estimated attendees Easter Sunday:
  2007: 541,314.
- Global Impact Goal—Number of attendees Easter Sunday:
  2017: 1,082,628.

Multicultural Ministries provided the following statistics for the North American Church:

- Number of culturally specific congregations, excluding Spanish and Black Evangelism Ministries, in North America:
  January 2008: 108
- Global Impact Goal—Number of culturally specific congregations in North America:
  December 2018: 216
- Number of culturally specific credentialed ministers, excluding Spanish and Black Evangelism Ministries, in North America:
  January 2008: 104
- Global Impact Goal—Number of culturally specific credentialed ministers in North America:
  December 2018: 208

Pastors will be asked to set goals and report results in the following areas annually:
- Number repented
- Number water baptized
- Number Spirit filled
- Easter Sunday attendance
- World Changers (Home Bible study teachers)

Global Impact Kickoff

It was determined that January 1, 2008, would be the kickoff date for Global Impact. It was also determined that, along with the goal of doubling in ten years, we would introduce three aspects of evangelism and promotion designed to get the program "up-and-running." The three areas that we decided to focus on in the beginning are Prayer and Fasting, My Family, and World Changers.

30 Days of Prayer and Fasting

Years ago I heard evangelist Michael Meadows say, "Where there is much prayer, there is much power. Where there is little prayer, there is little power. Where there is no prayer, there is no power."

Everyone involved in the planning of Global Impact agreed that we should begin with prayer and fasting. On January 6, the first Sunday of 2008, through February 4, the entire worldwide fellowship joined together to beseech heaven on behalf of reaching our world with the gospel. God will answer!

If your congregation did not participate in 30 Days of Prayer and Fasting during the month of January 2008, let me urge you to schedule a time of prayer and fasting as soon as possible.

Minister and Spouse Prayer Day

At the district level, the general superintendent asked all the district superintendents to call a day of prayer in their districts in conjunction with 30 Days of Prayer and Fasting. The purpose is to bring all district ministers and spouses together for corporate prayer for revival and unity.

My Family

I feel it is very important that we reinforce the doctrine for our own children and teenagers.
–Kenneth F. Haney

All United Pentecostal Church International families are asked to teach a Bible study in their own home, to their own family. Saving our own family and building a Bible foundation for our Apostolic children and youth is a high priority of Global Impact.

By taking deliberate steps to indoctrinate our children, the doctrine and its distinction will be sound in the hearts of the next generation. And, we will protect the United Pentecostal Church International against becoming just another religious organization. The Pentecostal Publishing House (*www.pentecostalpublishinghouse.com*) has many Bible study tools to choose from. Also, I have written a four-week Bible study that I am happy to make available—e-mail me at *BWCSrPastor@aol.com* to request your copy.

Mark Foster (*RevMFoster@aol.com*) and Wayne Huntley (*info.raleighupc@embarqmail.com*) serve as co-chairmen of this initiative.

World Changers

In response to the great commission, the United Pentecostal Church International is embarking on an aggressive evangelism campaign. The goal is to recruit 10,000 volunteers (World Changers), all ages, male and female, and all cultures, to teach one Bible study per week for 52 weeks, resulting in 520,000 Bible studies being taught in one year. To reach the goal of 10,000 World Changers, we need at least two volunteers per church in North America.

Volunteer home Bible study teachers should register at *www.GlobalImpactUPCI.com*. The Pentecostal Publishing House (*www.pentecostalpublishing.com*) has many Bible study tools to choose from.

Marrell Cornwell (*cbjmc@fpcwichita.org*) is the chairman of this evangelistic initiative.

Global Impact and the Local Congregation

When Global Impact was presented during the 2007 General Conference in Tampa, Florida, I was very pleased with the response of the pastors and ministers. Many of them immediately made a commitment to participate. Hundreds more have telephoned, sent e-mail, and viewed the Global Impact Web site for more information.

A number of contacts have asked the same question: "What steps should we take to get started?" Below I have listed simple steps for starting Global Impact within the local church.

Appoint a Local Church Global Impact Director

Your church's participation in Global Impact will be significantly enhanced if the pastor will appoint a Global Impact director to assist in all aspects of planning, implementation, promotion, and follow-up.

The director's job responsibilities could be to

1. assist the pastor in planning, implementing and promoting Global Impact within the local church;
2. maintain accurate records of the number water-baptized, and the number filled with the Holy Ghost annually;
3. maintain accurate records of annual Easter Sunday attendances;
4. complete and mail the annual Global Impact report;
5. aggressively promote the goals of Global Impact within the local church;
6. assist the pastor with all aspects of Global Impact.

Bishop Haney has suggested that the pastor's wife would make a great Global Impact director.

Set Local Church Goals

- Set your attendance goal for Easter Sunday 2008 (should be at least 7.2 percent more than Easter Sunday 2007 attendance).
- Set your goal for number of people to be water- and Spirit-baptized in 2008.

- Set goal for number of World Changers (home Bible study teachers). Remember, with only two to three volunteers per church in North America, we will reach the goal of 10,000 volunteers.
- Set goals for number of families that will participate in the My Family indoctrination initiative—which is, all families teaching a home Bible study to their own family, in their own home.

Passports

Every pastor should take the time necessary to work through the Pastors/Leaders Action Plan when it arrives. This booklet was designed to assist pastors and leaders in setting goals for their local congregation.

Pastors should also order enough Members Global Impact Passports for their congregants. As soon as possible, during one of the main services, hand out the passports to members and review them page-by-page. Encourage members to place the passports in their Bibles and carry them with them throughout the year.

Reporting

The reporting process is easy. Pastors will be asked to report the following statistics annually:
1. Easter Sunday attendance
2. Number water-baptized
3. Number filled with the Holy Ghost
This task can be delegated to the Global Impact director.

Customize Global Impact for Your Local Church

Feel free to customize Global Impact for your local church. For example, I am pastor at Bible World Church in Chesapeake, Virginia. We are going to promote "Chesapeake Impact" within our local church. Make it your own!

Conclusion

Our chance to impact people around the globe begins with a determined involvement to grow the local church. The United Pentecostal Church International grows from the grass roots up. For example, every home and foreign missionary is a product of the local church; every dollar given to spread the gospel comes from the local church; every minister was saved, trained, and sent, in and by a local church. Thus, the most effective way to build the United Pentecostal Church International is to build strong local churches.

Our prayer is that every pastor and church will catch the vision of Global Impact. January 1, 2008 marked a new day for the United Pentecostal Church International! On that day we embarked upon a journey that will result in the doubling of the church—from the local church to the international body.

I believe the blessings of God are undoubtedly on His church and He will absolutely reward the unwavering faith and tireless efforts of His people who are committed to building the kingdom.

We have been presented with the opportunity to literally become the catalyst for worldwide revival. If you have ever had the desire to do something of global significance—make a commitment to Global Impact.

Other books by Kenneth F. Haney

One God, One World, One Church, One Vision
This book unveils the vision of Kenneth F. Haney for the United Pentecostal Church International. The author challenges the church to step through the open door for an unprecedented harvest of souls.

The Irresistible Wave of Revival Revelation Revolution
Kenneth F. Haney challenges the reader to catch the vision and ride the wave of God's opportunity. God wills His people to exercise their faith and possess the promise as He will provide new anointing that is reserved for this last hour.